I0470716

Congaree National Park
Visitor Study

Fall 2011

Natural Resource Report NPS/NRSS/EQD/NRR— 2012/607

Mystera Samuelson, Yen Le, Steven J. Hollenhorst

Visitor Services Project
Park Studies Unit
University of Idaho
Moscow, ID 83844-1139

December 2012

U.S. Department of the Interior
National Park Service
Natural Resource Stewardship and Science
Fort Collins, Colorado

The National Park Service, Natural Resource Stewardship and Science office in Fort Collins, Colorado, publishes a range of reports that address natural resource topics. These reports are of interest and applicability to a broad audience in the National Park Service and others in natural resource management, including scientists, conservation and environmental constituencies, and the public.

The Natural Resource Report Series is used to disseminate high-priority, current natural resource management information with managerial application. The series targets a general, diverse audience, and may contain NPS policy considerations or address sensitive issues of management applicability.

All manuscripts in the series receive the appropriate level of peer review to ensure that the information is scientifically credible, technically accurate, appropriately written for the intended audience, and designed and published in a professional manner.

Data in this report were collected and analyzed using methods based on established, peer-reviewed protocols and were analyzed and interpreted within the guidelines of the protocols.

Views, statements, findings, conclusions, recommendations, and data in this report do not necessarily reflect views and policies of the National Park Service, U.S. Department of the Interior. Mention of trade names or commercial products does not constitute endorsement or recommendation for use by the U.S. Government.

This report is available from the Social Science Division (http://www.nature.nps.gov/socialscience/index.cfm) and the Natural Resource Publications Management website (http://www.nature.nps.gov/publications/nrpm/).

This report and other reports by the Visitor Services Project (VSP) are available from the VSP website (http://www.psu.uidaho.edu/c5/vsp/vsp-reports/) or by contacting the VSP office at (208) 885-7863.

Please cite this publication as:

Samuelson, M., Y. Le, and S. J. Hollenhorst. 2012. Congaree National Park visitor study: Fall 2011. Natural Resource Report NPS/NRSS/EQD/NRR—2012/607. National Park Service, Fort Collins, Colorado.

NPS 178/119304, December 2012

Contents

Contents (continued)

Executive Summary

This visitor study report profiles a systematic random sample of Congaree National Park (NP) visitors during October 27 – November 27, 2011. This study was conducted with a systematic, random sample of visitor groups that arrived at the park visitor center. The group respondent completed a mail-back questionnaire after their visit. A total of 452 questionnaires were distributed to visitor groups. Of those, 329 questionnaires were returned, resulting in a 72.8% response rate.

Group size and type

Forty-nine percent of visitor groups consisted of two people. Sixty-three percent of visitor groups consisted of family groups.

State or country of residence

United States visitors were from 33 states and Washington, DC and comprised 98% of total visitation during the survey period, with 49% from South Carolina. International visitors were from four countries, although there were too few respondents to provide reliable data.

Frequency of visits

Seventy-four percent of visitors visited the park once in the past 12 months and 62% were visiting the park for the first time in their lifetime. Eighteen percent had visited five or more times in their lifetime.

Age, ethnicity, race, and educational level

Thirty-two percent of visitors were ages 56-70 years, 23% were 21-40 years, 17% were ages 15 years or younger, and 6% were 71 or older. Two percent of visitors were Hispanic or Latino. Most visitors (95%) were White and 2% were African American. Forty-two percent of respondents had completed a bachelor's degree and 33% had a graduate degree.

Physical conditions

Six percent of visitor groups had members with physical conditions affecting their ability to access or participate in activities and services.

Awareness of park programs

Sixty-one percent of visitor groups were aware, prior to their visit, of the various programs offered at the park.

Knowledge of Congressionally designated wilderness

Fifty-eight percent of respondents indicated they were aware of what congressionally designated wilderness is, before visiting the park. Forty-six percent of visitor groups said they learned about wilderness while at the park.

Non-native species management

Fifty-four percent of respondents were aware of the policy regarding removal of non-native species. Most visitor groups (90%) were in support of removal of non-native plants and 77% were supportive of removal of non-native animals.

Scientific research and education in the park

Forty-nine percent of visitor groups noticed scientists working or scientific markers or equipment being used in the park. Through programs or products, 26% of the visitors learned about the results of scientific studies conducted at the park.

Information sources

Most visitors (92%) obtained information about the park prior to their visit. Of those visitors, 51% used the park website and 28% obtained their information from friends/relatives/word of mouth.

Park as destination

Many visitor groups (75%) said the park was their primary destination and 23% said it was one of several destinations.

Executive Summary (continued)

Primary reason for visiting the area
Thirty-one percent of visitor groups were residents of the area (within a 1-hour drive of the park). The most common primary reason for visiting the park area among nonresident visitor groups was to visit the park (66%).

Overnight stays
Forty percent of visitor groups stayed overnight away from home either in the park or the area. Of those visitors that stayed outside the park (within a 1-hour drive), 52% stayed one night and 21% stayed two nights.

Accommodations
Of those visitor groups that stayed outside the park (within 1-hour drive), 71% stayed in a lodge, hotel, motel, cabin, rented condo/home, or B&B.

Time spent at park and in the area
The average length of stay in the park was 9.6 hours. The average length of stay in the area was 50 hours, or 2.1 days.

Activities
The most common visitor activities within the park were walking/hiking (85%) and visiting the visitor center (74%).

Use of park trails
The Elevated Boardwalk Trail was used by 81% of visitor groups and the Low Boardwalk Trail was used by 63%.

Information services and facilities
The information services and facilities most commonly used by visitor groups were park brochure/map (87%), assistance from park staff (83%), and visitor center exhibits (77%).

Visitor services and facilities
The visitor services and facilities most commonly used by visitor groups were boardwalks (91%), restrooms (90%), and parking areas (88%).

Protecting park attributes, resources, and experiences
The highest combined proportions of "extremely important" and "very important" ratings of protecting park resources and attributes, included clean water (94%), clean air (93%), and natural quiet/sounds of nature (92%).

Elements affecting park experience
Forty percent of visitor groups experienced airplane noise, and of those, 42% felt it detracted from their park experience. Eighty-nine percent of visitor groups experienced small numbers of visitors on trails, of which 38% felt this added to their park experience.

Expenditures
The average visitor group expenditure (inside and outside the park within a 1-hour drive) was $181. The median group expenditure (50% of groups spent more and 50% of groups spent less) was $52. The average total expenditure per capita was $75.

Future visit
Regarding future organized activities/programs of interest, visitor groups preferred canoeing/kayaking (65%) and the night walk/night sky program (57%). The most often preferred future topics to learn about were plants and animals (71%) and champion trees (63%).

Overall quality
Most visitor groups (98%) rated the overall quality of facilities, services, and recreational opportunities at Congaree NP as "very good" or "good." No visitor groups rated the overall quality as "very poor."

For more information about the Visitor Services Project, please contact the Park Studies Unit at the University of Idaho at (208) 885-7863 or the following website http://www.psu.uidaho.edu.

Acknowledgements

We thank Mystera Samuelson for compiling the report, Lauren Gurniewicz for overseeing the fieldwork, the staff and volunteers of Congaree NP for assisting with the survey, and David Vollmer and Matthew Strawn for data processing.

About the Authors

Mystera Samuelson was a research assistant for the Visitor Services Project. Yen Le, Ph.D., is Assistant Director of the Visitor Services Project at the University of Idaho, and Steven Hollenhorst, Ph.D., was the Director of the Park Studies Unit, Department of Conservation Social Sciences, University of Idaho.

Introduction

This report describes the results of a visitor study at Congaree National Park (NP) in Hopkins, SC, conducted October 27 – November 27, 2011 by the National Park Service (NPS) Visitor Services Project (VSP), part of the Park Studies Unit (PSU) at the University of Idaho.

As described in the National Park Service website for Congaree National Park: "Welcome to the largest remnant of old-growth floodplain forest remaining on the continent! Experience champion trees, towering to record size amidst astonishing biodiversity…Congaree National Park houses a museum quality exhibit area within the Harry Hampton Visitor Center, a 2.4 mile boardwalk loop trail, over 20 miles of backwoods hiking trails, canoeing, kayaking, fishing and more…As a designated Wilderness area, International Biosphere Reserve, Globally Important Bird Area, and the largest intact tract of old-growth floodplain forest in North America, Congaree National Park is home to a variety of ongoing research and education projects." (http://www.nps.gov/cong/index.htm, retrieved October, 2011).

Organization of the Report

This report is organized into three sections.

Section 1: **Methods**
This section discusses the procedures, limitations, and special conditions that may affect the study results.

Section 2: **Results**
This section provides a summary for each question in the questionnaire and includes visitor comments to open-ended questions. The presentation of the results of this study does not follow the order of questions in the questionnaire.

Section 3: **Appendices**
Appendix 1: *The Questionnaire*. A copy of the questionnaire distributed to visitor groups.

Appendix 2: *Additional Analysis*. A list of sample questions for cross-references and cross comparisons. Comparisons can be analyzed within a park or between parks. Results of additional analyses are not included in this report.

Appendix 3: *Decision Rules for Checking Nonresponse Bias*. An explanation of how the nonresponse bias was determined.

Presentation of the Results

Results are represented in the form of graphs (see Example 1), scatter plots, pie charts, tables, and text.

Key

Example 1

1. The figure title describes the graph's information.

2. Listed above the graph, the "N" shows the number of individuals or visitor groups responding to the question. If "N" is less than 30, "**CAUTION!**" is shown on the graph to indicate the results may be unreliable.

 * appears when the total percentages do not equal 100 due to rounding.

** appears when total percentages do not equal 100 because visitors could select more than one answer choice.

3. Vertical information describes the response categories.

4. Horizontal information shows the number or proportion of responses in each category.

5. In most graphs, percentages provide additional information.

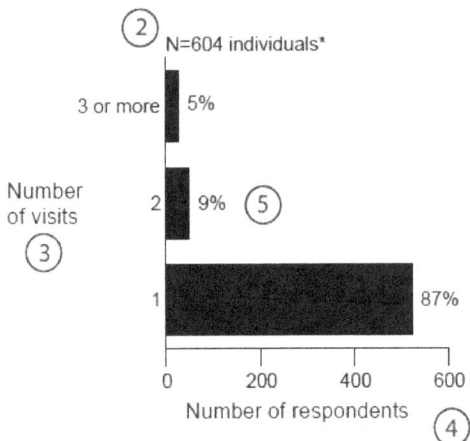

Figure 14. Number of visits to the park in past 12 months

Methods

Survey Design and Procedures

Sample size and sampling plan

All VSP questionnaires follow design principles outlined in Don A. Dillman's book *Mail and Internet Surveys: The Tailored Design Method* (2007). Using this method, the sample size was calculated based on park visitation statistics of previous years.

Brief interviews were conducted with a systematic, random sample of visitor groups that arrived at the visitor center during October 27 – November 27, 2011. Visitors were surveyed between the hours of 8 a.m. and 5 p.m. During this survey, 480 visitor groups were contacted and 452 of these groups (94%) accepted questionnaires. (The average acceptance rate for 250 VSP visitor studies conducted from 1988 through 2011 is 91.5%.) Questionnaires were completed and returned by 329 respondents, resulting in a 72.8% response rate for this study. (The average response rate for the 250 VSP visitor studies is 72.3%).

Questionnaire design

The Congaree NP questionnaire was developed at a workshop held with park staff to design and prioritize questions. Some of the questions were comparable with VSP studies conducted at other parks while others were customized for Congaree NP. Many questions asked visitors to choose answers from a list of responses, often with an open-ended option, while others were completely open-ended.

No pilot study was conducted to test the Congaree NP questionnaire. However, all questions followed Office Management and Budget (OMB) guidelines and/or were used in previous surveys; thus, the clarity and consistency of the survey instrument have been tested and supported.

Survey procedure

Visitor groups were greeted, briefly introduced to the purpose of the study, and asked to participate. If visitors agreed, they were asked which member (at least 16 years old) had the next birthday. The individual with the next birthday was selected to complete the questionnaire for the group. An interview, lasting approximately two minutes, was conducted with that person to determine group size, group type, age of the member completing the questionnaire, and how this visit to the park fit into their group's travel plans. These individuals were asked their names, addresses, and telephone numbers or email addresses in order to mail a reminder/thank-you postcard and follow-ups. Participants were asked to complete the questionnaire after their visit and return it in the Business Reply Mail envelope provided.

Two weeks following the survey, a reminder/thank-you postcard was mailed to all participants who provided a valid mailing address (see Table 1). Replacement questionnaires were mailed to participants who had not returned their questionnaires four weeks after the survey. Seven weeks after the survey, a second round of replacement questionnaires was mailed to participants who had not returned their questionnaires.

Table 1. Follow-up mailing distribution

Round	Mailing	Date	U.S.	International	Total
1	Postcards	November 23, 2011	218	6	224
1	1st replacement	December 12, 2011	97	3	100
1	2nd replacement	January 3, 2012	94	0	94
2	Postcards	December 12, 2011	178	0	178
2	1st replacement	December 23, 2011	76	0	76
2	2nd replacement	January 18, 2012	58	0	58

Data analysis

Returned questionnaires were coded and the responses were processed using custom and standard statistical software applications—Statistical Analysis Software® (SAS), and a custom designed FileMaker Pro® application. Descriptive statistics and cross-tabulations were calculated for the coded data; responses to open-ended questions were categorized and summarized. Double-key data entry validation was performed on numeric and text entry variables and the remaining checkbox (bubble) variables were read by optical mark recognition (OMR) software.

Limitations

As with all surveys, this study has limitations that should be considered when interpreting the results.

1. This was a self-administered survey. Respondents completed the questionnaire after the visit, which may have resulted in poor recall. Thus, it is not possible to know whether visitor responses reflected actual behavior.

2. The data reflect visitor use patterns at the selected sites during the study period of October 27 – November 27, 2011. The results present a 'snapshot in time' and do not necessarily apply to visitors during other times of the year.

3. Caution is advised when interpreting any data with a sample size of less than 30, as the results may be unreliable. Whenever the sample size is less than 30, the word **"CAUTION!"** is included in the graph, figure, table, or text.

4. Occasionally, there may be inconsistencies in the results. Inconsistencies arise from missing data or incorrect answers (due to misunderstood directions, carelessness, or poor recall of information). Therefore, refer to both the percentage and N (number of individuals or visitor groups) when interpreting the results.

Special conditions

The weather during the survey period was generally sunny and cool with occasional cloud cover. Temperatures ranged from 60 to 80 F. No special events occurred in the area that would have affected the type and amount of visitation to the park.

Checking nonresponse bias

Four variables were used to check nonresponse bias: participant age, group size, group type, and how park fit in to travel plans. Due to large number of missing zip codes, distance from home to the park was not used to test non-response bias. Respondents and nonrespondents were not significantly different in all variables except for average age (see Tables 2 - 4). The results indicated that respondents at younger age ranges (especially 40 and younger) may be underrepresented in the results. See Appendix 3 for more details of the nonresponse bias checking procedures.

Table 2. Comparison of respondents and nonrespondents by average age and group size

Variable	Respondents	Nonrespondents	p-value (t-test)
Age (years)	51.18 (N=328)	43.47 (N=123)	<0.001
Group size	2.75 (N=324)	3.74 (N=120)	0.353

Table 3. Comparison of respondents and nonrespondents by group type

Group type	Respondents	Nonrespondents	p-value (chi-square)
Alone	48 (15%)	21 (5%)	
Family	204 (63%)	69 (15%)	
Friends	47 (15%)	27 (6%)	
Family and friends	23 (7%)	4 (1%)	
Other	2 (1%)	0 (0%)	
			0.139

Table 4. Comparison of respondents and nonrespondents by how park fit in to travel plans

Destination	Respondents	Nonrespondents	p-value (chi-square)
Park as primary destination	232 (75%)	99 (22%)	
Park as one of several destinations	81 (23%)	19 (4%)	
Unplanned visit	9 (3%)	4 (1%)	
			0.097

6

Results

Group and Visitor Characteristics

Visitor group size

Question 19b
On this visit, how many people were in your personal group, including yourself?

Results
- 49% of visitor groups consisted of two people (see Figure 1).

- 17% were alone.

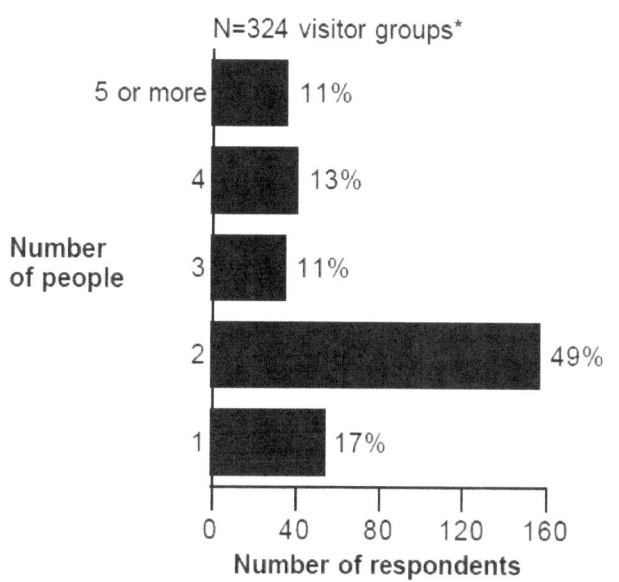

Figure 1. Visitor group size

Visitor group type

Question 19a
On this visit, what kind of personal group (not guided tour/school/other organized group) were you with?

Results
- 63% of visitor groups consisted of family members (see Figure 2).

- "Other" group types (1%) were:

    Club Atlanta Outdoor Club
    Co-workers

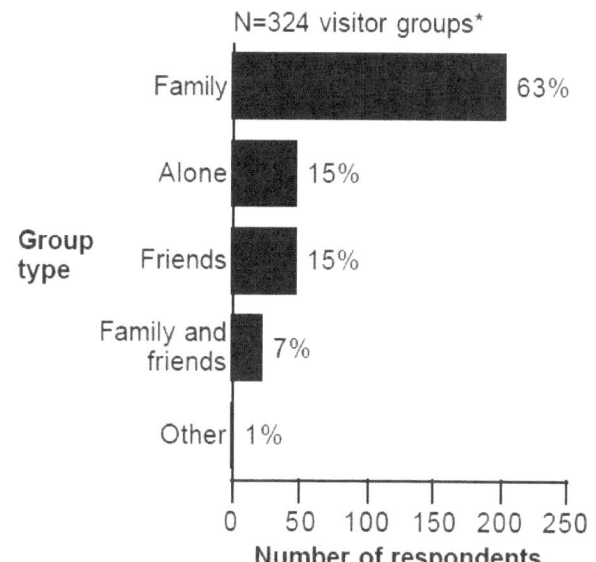

Figure 2. Visitor group type

---

*total percentages do not equal 100 due to rounding

**total percentages do not equal 100 because visitors could select more than one answer

Visitors with organized groups

Question 18a
On this visit, were you and your personal group with a commercial guided tour group?

Results
- 1% of visitor groups were with a commercial guided tour group (see Figure 3).

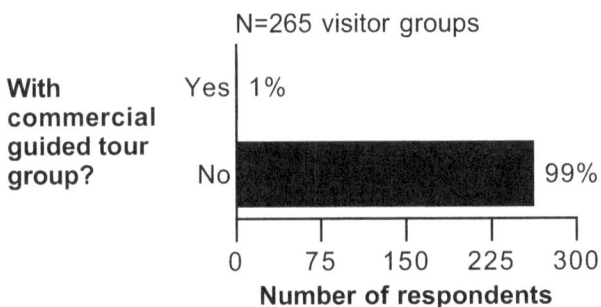

Figure 3. Visitors with a commercial guided tour group

Question 18b
On this visit, were you and your personal group with a school/ educational group?

Results
- 3% of visitor groups were with a school/educational group (see Figure 4).

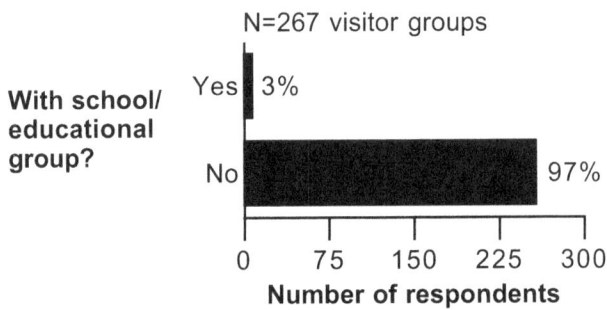

Figure 4. Visitors with a school/educational group

Question 18c
On this visit, were you and your personal group with an "other" organized group (scouts, work, church, etc.)?

Results
- 7% of visitor groups were with an "other" organized group (see Figure 5).

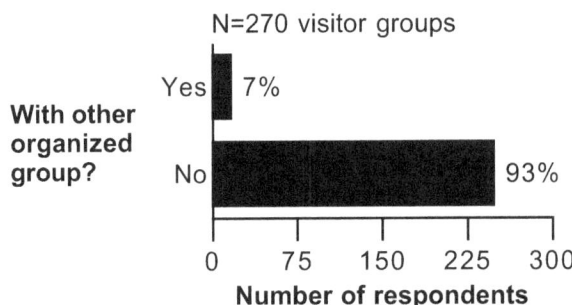

Figure 5. Visitors with an "other" organized group

*total percentages do not equal 100 due to rounding
**total percentages do not equal 100 because visitors could select more than one answer

Question 18d
If you were with one of these organized groups, how many people, including yourself, were in this group?

Results – Interpret with **CAUTION!**
- Not enough visitor groups responded to this question to provide reliable results (see Figure 6).

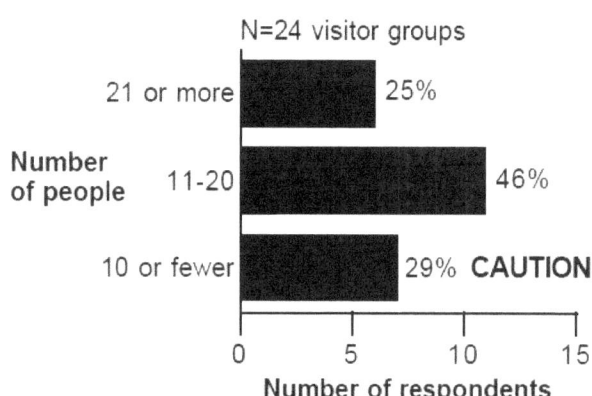

Figure 6. Organized group size

---

*total percentages do not equal 100 due to rounding
**total percentages do not equal 100 because visitors could select more than one answer

United States visitors by state of residence

Question 20b

For you and your personal group on this visit, what is your state of residence?

Note: Response was limited to 7 members from each visitor group.

Results

- U.S. visitors were from 33 states and Washington, DC and comprised 98% of total visitation to the park during the survey period.

- 49% of U.S. visitors came from South Carolina (see Table 5 and Figure 7).

- 9% came from North Carolina and 5% were from Georgia.

- Smaller proportions came from 30 other states and Washington, DC.

Table 5. United States visitors by state of residence

State	Number of visitors	Percent of U.S. visitors N=775 individuals*	Percent of total visitors N=791 individuals
South Carolina	381	49%	48%
North Carolina	70	9%	9%
Georgia	35	5%	4%
Florida	31	4%	4%
Pennsylvania	26	3%	3%
Michigan	24	3%	3%
Tennessee	18	2%	2%
Ohio	15	2%	2%
Virginia	15	2%	2%
Maryland	14	2%	2%
New York	14	2%	2%
Washington	14	2%	2%
Illinois	12	2%	2%
California	11	1%	1%
Wisconsin	10	1%	1%
18 other states and Washington, DC	85	11%	11%

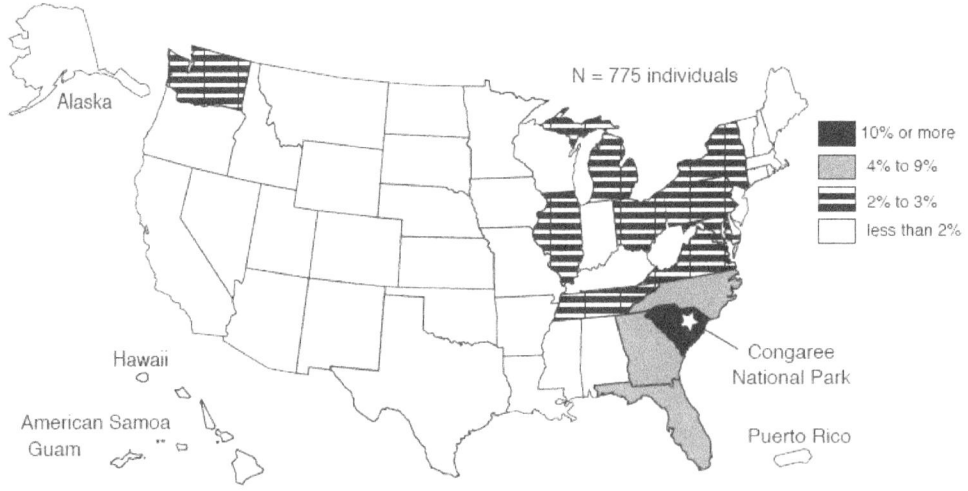

Figure 7. United States visitors by state of residence

---

*total percentages do not equal 100 due to rounding

**total percentages do not equal 100 because visitors could select more than one answer

Visitors from South Carolina and adjacent states by county of residence

Note: Response was limited to 7 members from each visitor group.

Results

- Visitors from South Carolina and adjacent states were from 51 counties and comprised 62% of the total U.S. visitation to the park during the survey period.

- 28% came from Richland County, SC (see Table 6).

- 21% Came from Lexington County, SC.

- Smaller proportions of visitors came from 49 other counties in South Carolina and adjacent states.

Table 6. Visitors from South Carolina and adjacent states by county of residence

County, State	Number of visitors N=481 individuals	Percent*
Richland, SC	136	28
Lexington, SC	104	21
Mecklenburg, NC	20	4
Greenville, SC	17	4
Charleston, SC	13	3
Sumter, SC	12	2
Anderson, SC	11	2
Oconee, SC	10	2
Beaufort, SC	9	2
Floyd, GA	8	2
Berkeley, SC	7	1
Newberry, SC	7	1
Orangeburg, SC	7	1
Buncombe, NC	6	1
Gaston, NC	6	1
Horry, SC	6	1
Kershaw, SC	6	1
Spartanburg, SC	6	1
Barnwell, SC	5	1
Guilford, NC	5	1
Nash, NC	5	1
30 other counties	75	16

*total percentages do not equal 100 due to rounding

**total percentages do not equal 100 because visitors could select more than one answer

International visitors by country of residence

Question 20b

For you and your personal group on this visit, what is your country of residence?

Note: Response was limited to 7 members from each visitor group.

Results – CAUTION!

- Not enough visitors responded to this question to provide reliable results (see Table 7).

Table 7. International visitors by country of residence – **CAUTION!**

Country	Number of visitors	Percent of international visitors N=16 individuals*	Percent of total visitors N=791 individuals
Australia	8	50%	1%
Canada	3	19%	<1%
Germany	3	19%	<1%
United Kingdom	2	13%	<1%

*total percentages do not equal 100 due to rounding
**total percentages do not equal 100 because visitors could select more than one answer

Number of visits to Congaree NP in past 12 months

Question 20c
    For you and your personal group on this visit, how many times have you visited Congaree NP in the past 12 months (including this visit)?

Note: Response was limited to 7 members from each visitor group.

Results
 •   74% of visitors visited the park once in the past 12 months (see Figure 8).

 •   12% of visitors visited two times.

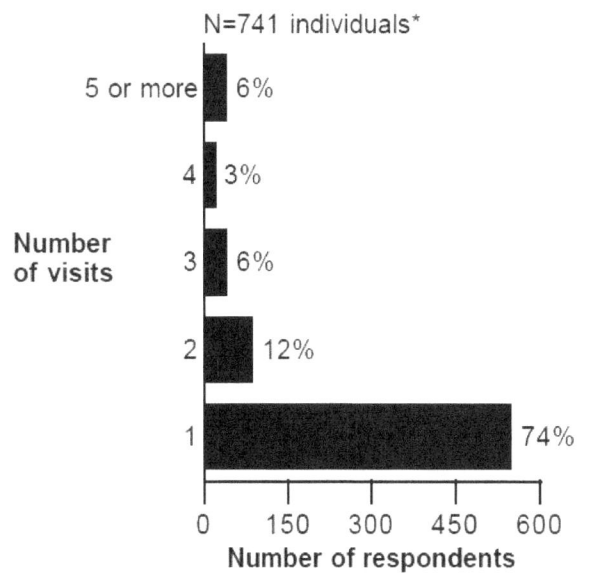

Figure 8. Number of visits to park in past 12 months

Number of lifetime visits to Congaree NP

Question 20d
    For you and your personal group on this visit, how many times have you visited Congaree NP in your lifetime (including this visit)?

Note: Response was limited to 7 members from each visitor group.

Results
 •   62% of visitors visited the park once in their lifetime (see Figure 9).

 •   18% of visitors visited five or more times.

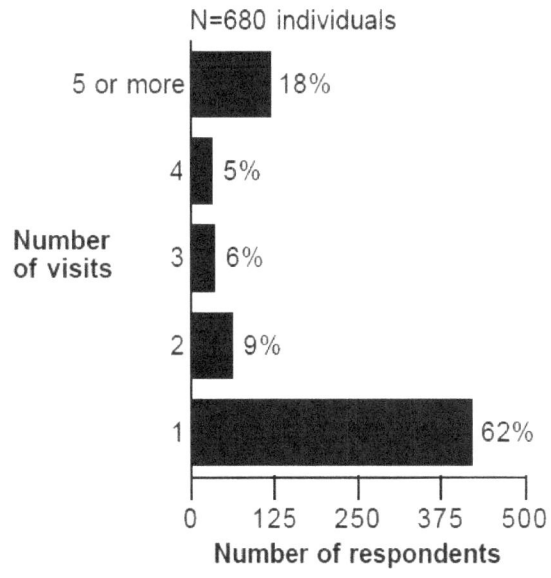

Figure 9. Number of visits to park in lifetime

---

*total percentages do not equal 100 due to rounding
**total percentages do not equal 100 because visitors could select more than one answer

Number of visits to other national parks in past 12 months

Question 20e

For you and your personal group on this visit, how many times have you visited other national parks in the past 12 months (including this visit)?

Note: Response was limited to 7 members from each visitor group.

Results

- 27% of visitors had visited other national parks once in the past 12 months (see Figure 10).

- 25% had visited other national parks five or more times.

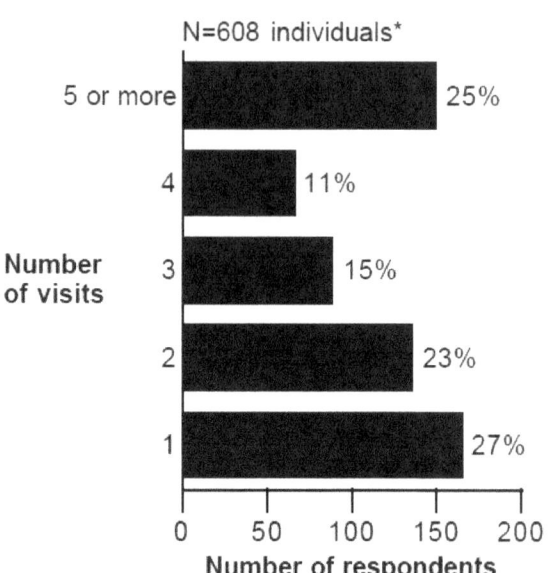

Figure 10. Number of visits to other national parks in past 12 months

Number of lifetime visits to other national parks

Question 20f

For you and your personal group on this visit, how many times have you visited other national parks in your lifetime (including this visit)?

Note: Response was limited to 7 members from each visitor group.

Results

- 69% of visitors had visited other national parks six or more times in their lifetime (see Figure 11).

- 8% of visitors had visited another national park once in their lifetime.

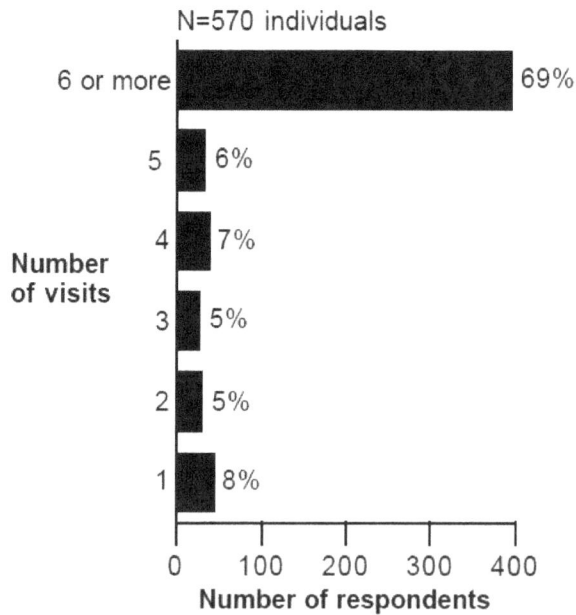

Figure 11. Number of visits to other national parks in lifetime

*total percentages do not equal 100 due to rounding

**total percentages do not equal 100 because visitors could select more than one answer

14

Visitor age

Question 20a

For you and your personal group on this visit, what is your current age?

Note: Response was limited to 7 members from each visitor group.

Results

- Visitor ages ranged from one to 94 years.

- 41% were 51-70 years old (see Figure 12).

- 25% were 26-45 years old.

- 17% were 15 years or younger.

- 6% were 71 years or older.

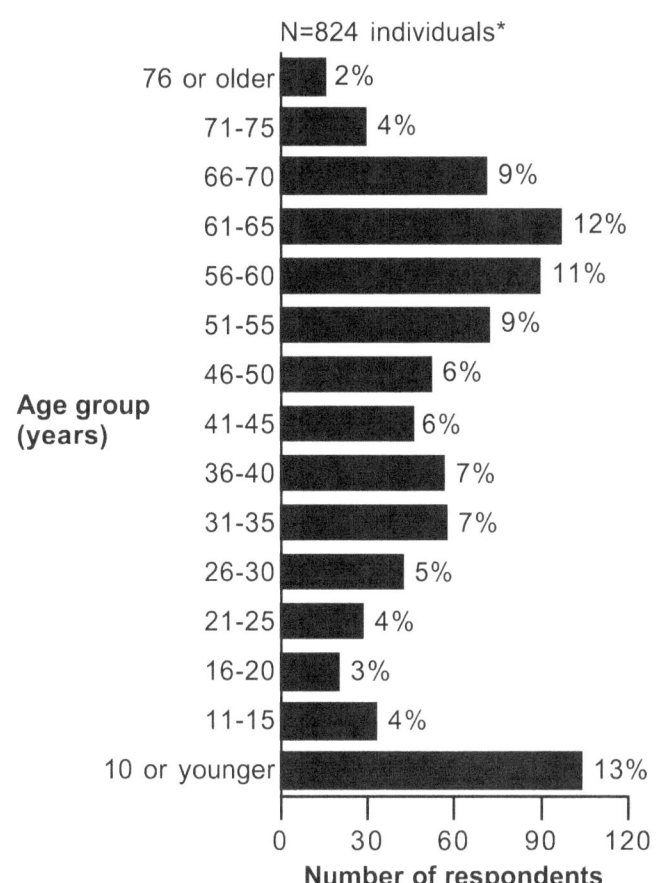

Figure 12. Visitor age

---

*total percentages do not equal 100 due to rounding

**total percentages do not equal 100 because visitors could select more than one answer

Visitor ethnicity

Question 23a

Are you or members of your personal group Hispanic or Latino?

Note: Response was limited to 7 members from each visitor group.

Results
- 2% of visitors were Hispanic or Latino (see Figure 13).

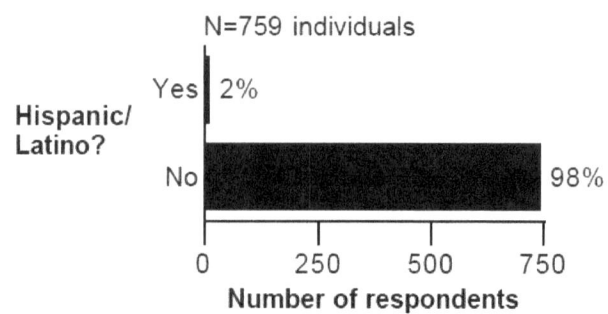

Figure 13. Visitors who were Hispanic or Latino

Visitor race

Question 23b

What is your race? What is the race of each member of your personal group?

Note: Response was limited to 7 members from each visitor group.

Results
- 95% of visitors were White (see Figure 14).

- 2% were Black or African American.

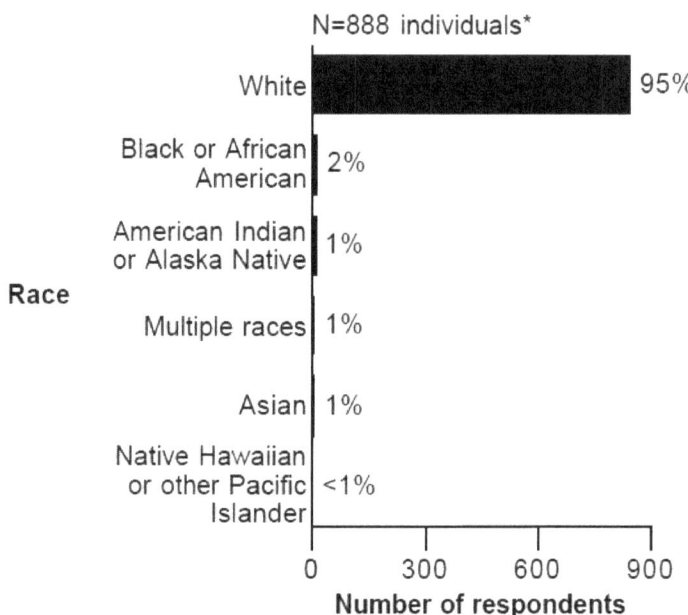

Figure 14. Visitor race

---

*total percentages do not equal 100 due to rounding

**total percentages do not equal 100 because visitors could select more than one answer

Visitors with physical conditions affecting access/participation

Question 22a

Does anyone in your personal group have mobility or other physical impairments?

Results

- 6% of visitor groups had members with mobility or other physical conditions (see Figure 15).

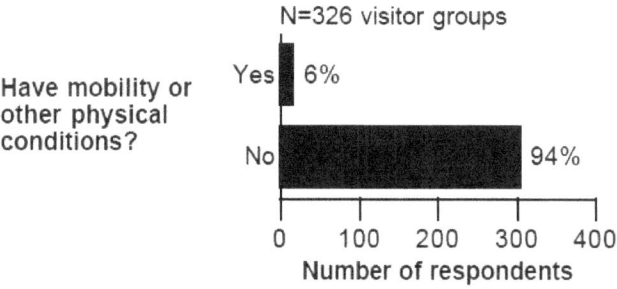

Figure 15. Visitor groups that had members with mobility or other physical conditions

Question 22b

If YES, did anyone in your personal group have a physical condition that made it difficult to access or participate in park activities or services?

Results – Interpret with **CAUTION!**

- Not enough visitor groups responded to provide reliable results (see Figure 16).

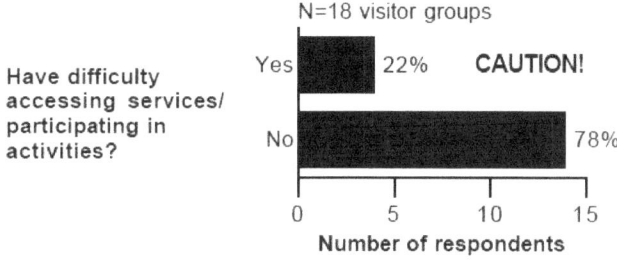

Figure 16. Visitor groups that had a member with physical conditions affecting access to services or participation in park activities

*total percentages do not equal 100 due to rounding
**total percentages do not equal 100 because visitors could select more than one answer

Respondent level of education

Question 21
For you only, what is the highest level of education you have completed?

Results
- 42% of respondents had a bachelor's degree (see Figure 17).

- 33% had a graduate degree.

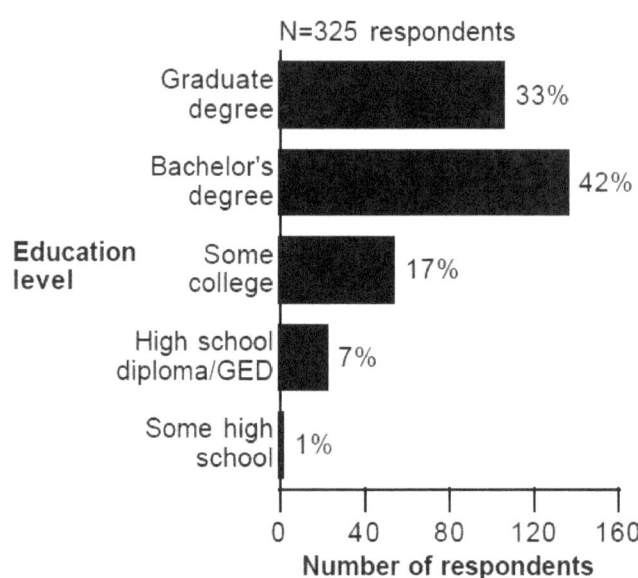

Figure 17. Respondent level of education

Respondent household income

Question 25a
Which category best represents
your annual household income?

Results
- 61% had an income
  between $50,000 and
  $149,999 (see Figure 18).

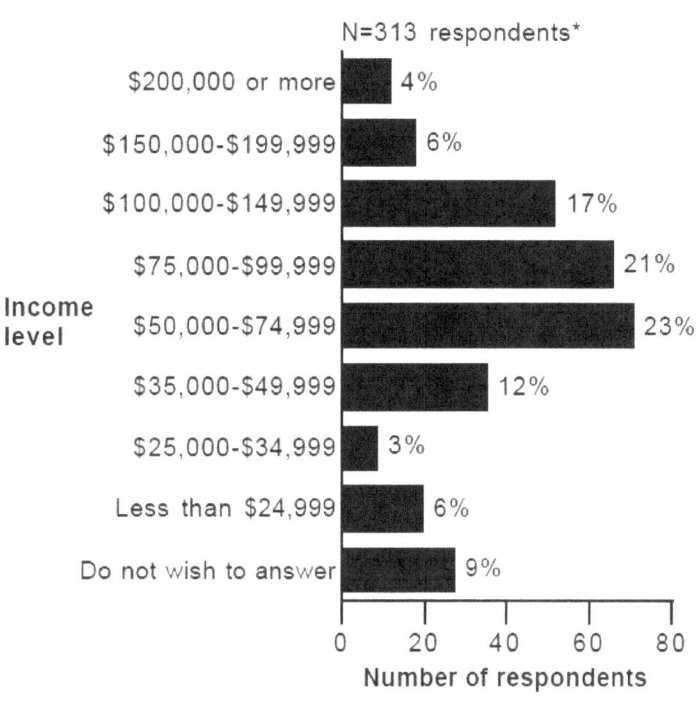

Figure 18. Respondent household level of income

Respondent household size

Question 25b
How many people are in your
household?

Results
- 48% of respondents had
  two people in their
  household (see Figure 19).

- 18% had one person in
  their household.

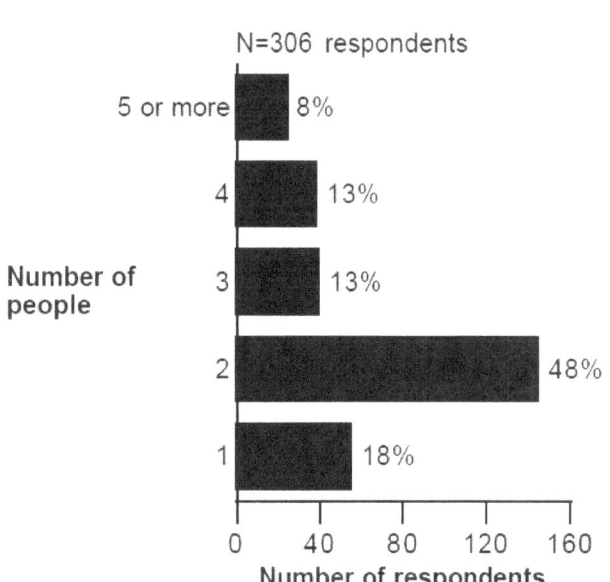

Figure 19. Number of people in respondent household

---

*total percentages do not equal 100 due to rounding

**total percentages do not equal 100 because visitors could select more than one answer

Awareness of park programs

Question 2
　　Prior to your visit, were you and your personal group aware of programs (ranger-led walks, canoe trips, presentations, school group tours, etc.) offered in Congaree NP?

Results
　　• 61% of visitor groups were aware of programs offered at the park (see Figure 20).

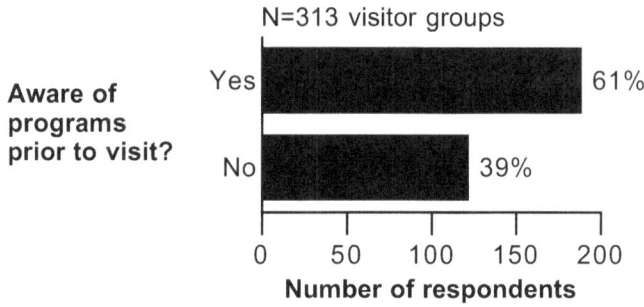

Figure 20. Visitor groups that were aware of programs in Congaree NP

---

*total percentages do not equal 100 due to rounding
**total percentages do not equal 100 because visitors could select more than one answer

Park name change and decision to visit

Question 3a
In 2003, Congaree Swamp National Monument became Congaree NP. Did this name change have any effect on your decision to visit?

Results
• 17% of respondents said their decision to visit was affected by the name change (see Figure 21).

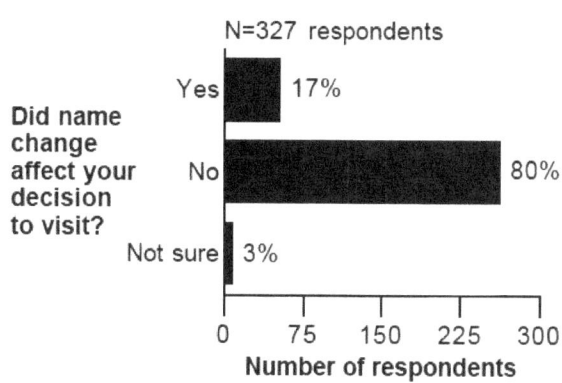

N=327 respondents

Figure 21. Respondents for whom the name change affected their decision to visit

Question 3b
If YES, what effect did it have?
(Open-ended)

Results
• 46 respondents commented on the effect of the park's name change (see Table 8.)

Table 8. Effect of name change on decision to visit
(N=56 comments; some visitor groups made more than one comment)

Comment	Number of times mentioned
Trying to visit all national parks	18
"National park" seems more important	5
Increased desire to visit	4
Glad there is a local national park	3
More likely to travel out of the way for a national park	2
More likely to visit a national park	2
Expect site and facility improvements	2
The title "national park" is more appealing	2
Designation increased media coverage	2
Always interested in visiting a national park	1
Association between national parks and recreation opportunities	1
Increased financial security	1
Increased importance placed on the swamp	1
More recognition for national park	1
National monument doesn't seem like a park, never wanted to visit	1
National park #1 Fan	1
National park seemed safer	1
"National parks" seemed more user friendly	1
National parks are special places	1
National parks have unique features	1
Other comments	5

*total percentages do not equal 100 due to rounding
**total percentages do not equal 100 because visitors could select more than one answer

Knowledge of congressionally designated wilderness

Question 4a
Prior to your visit, were you aware of what congressionally designated wilderness is?

Results
- 58% of respondents were aware of congressionally designated wilderness (see Figure 22).

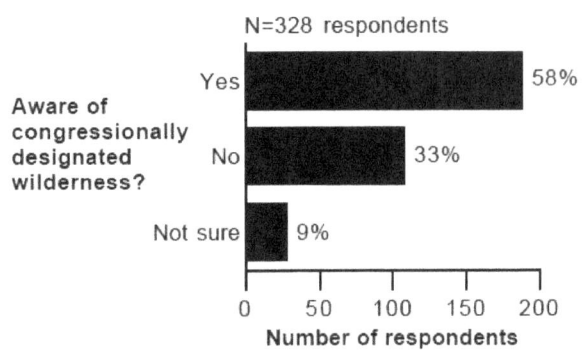

Figure 22. Respondents who were aware of congressionally designated wilderness

Question 4b
If NO, did you and your personal group learn about congressionally designated wilderness during your visit?

Results
- 46% of visitor groups said they learned about congressionally designated wilderness at Congaree NP during their visit (see Figure 23).

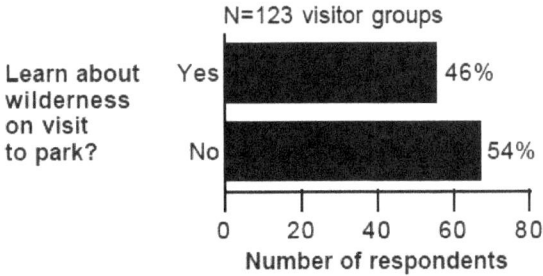

Figure 23. Visitor groups that learned about congressionally designated wilderness at park

Park policy to remove non-native species

Question 5
The National Park Service has a policy to control or remove non-native plants and animals from within park boundaries. Non-native species occupy an area that is not part of their natural, historic range, and often originated from another continent or region. Many of these species are invasive and damage park resources. Were you aware of this policy prior to your visit to Congaree NP?

Results
- 54% of respondents were aware of the park policy to remove non-native species (see Figure 24).

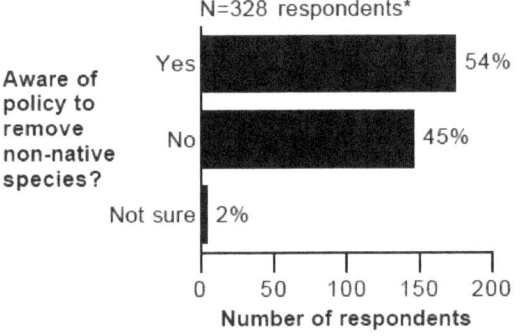

Figure 24. Respondents aware of park policy regarding non-native species

*total percentages do not equal 100 due to rounding

**total percentages do not equal 100 because visitors could select more than one answer

Support for policy to remove non-native species

Question 6

Would you and your personal group be supportive of the control and removal of non-native species at Congaree NP?

Results

- 90% of visitor groups were supportive of the removal of non-native plants (see Figure 25).

- 77% were supportive of the removal of non-native animals (see Figure 26).

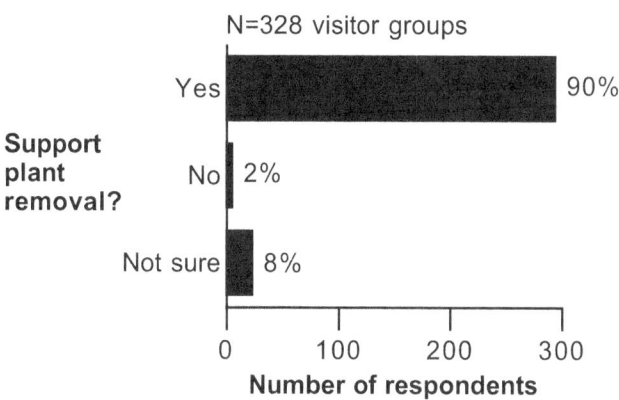

Figure 25. Visitor groups supporting the removal of non-native plants

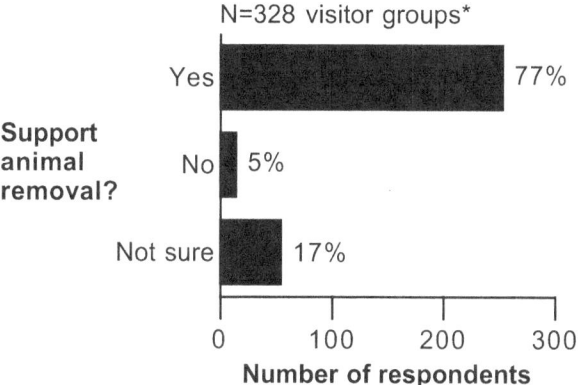

Figure 26. Visitor groups supporting the removal of non-native animals

*total percentages do not equal 100 due to rounding
**total percentages do not equal 100 because visitors could select more than one answer

Awareness of research and education in the park

Question 15a

Prior to this visit, were you and your personal group aware that Congaree NP is the home to the Old-Growth Bottomland Forest Research and Education Center, one of 21 centers nationwide?

Results

- 23% of visitor groups were aware of the Old-Growth Bottomland Forest Research and Education Center before their visit (see Figure 27).

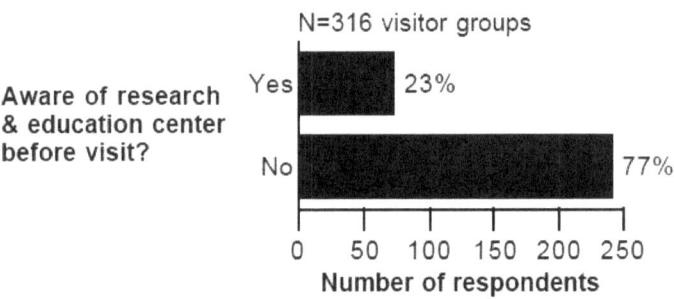

N=316 visitor groups

Figure 27. Visitor groups that were aware of the Old-Growth Bottomland Forest Research and Education Center before visit

Question 15b

Did you and your personal group notice any scientists, scientific markers, or scientific equipment at work while you were in the park?

Results

- 49% of visitor groups noticed scientists, scientific markers, or scientific equipment at work in the park (see Figure 28).

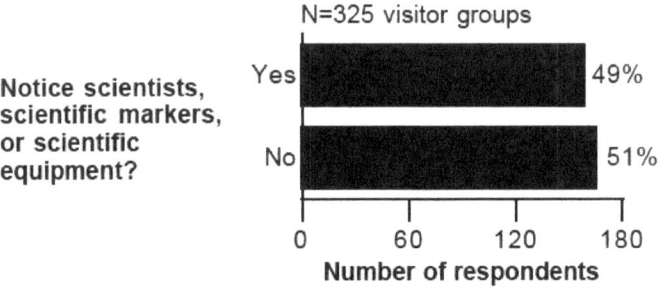

N=325 visitor groups

Figure 28. Visitor groups that noticed scientists, scientific markers, or scientific equipment at work during this visit

Question 15c

Did you and your personal group – through programs and products – learn about actual results of scientific studies at the park?

Results

- 26% of visitor groups learned about research results through programs and products while in the park (see Figure 29).

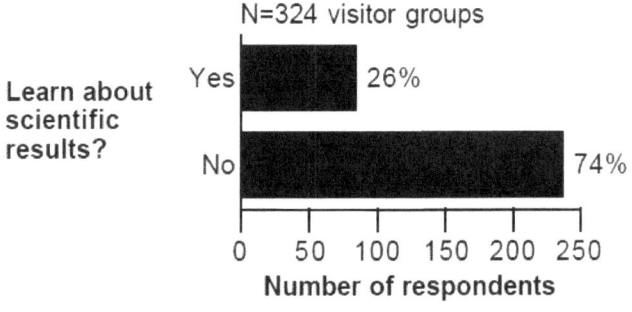

N=324 visitor groups

Figure 29. Visitor groups that learned about scientific results in the park

---

*total percentages do not equal 100 due to rounding

**total percentages do not equal 100 because visitors could select more than one answer

Trip/Visit Characteristics and Preferences

Information sources prior to visit

Question 1

Prior to your visit, how did you and your personal group obtain information about Congaree NP?

Results

- 92% of visitor groups obtained information about Congaree NP prior to their visit (see Figure 30).

- As shown in Figure 31, among those visitor groups that obtained information about Congaree NP prior to their visit, the most common sources were:

  51% Park website
  28% Friends/relatives/word of mouth
  25% Previous visits

- Other websites used (6%) were:

  columbia4kids.com
  google.com
  maps.google.com
  mapquest.com
  nps.gov
  peddlernet.com
  scan.com

- "Other" sources (7%) were:

  Bicycle group from Columbia
  Fort Jackson
  GPS
  Great Cypress Swamps book
  Joan Maloof book
  National Park Passport
  National Parks book
  Senior group trip
  South Carolina State Fair

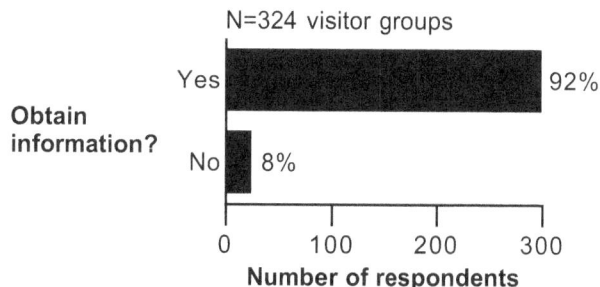

Figure 30. Visitor groups that obtained information prior to visit

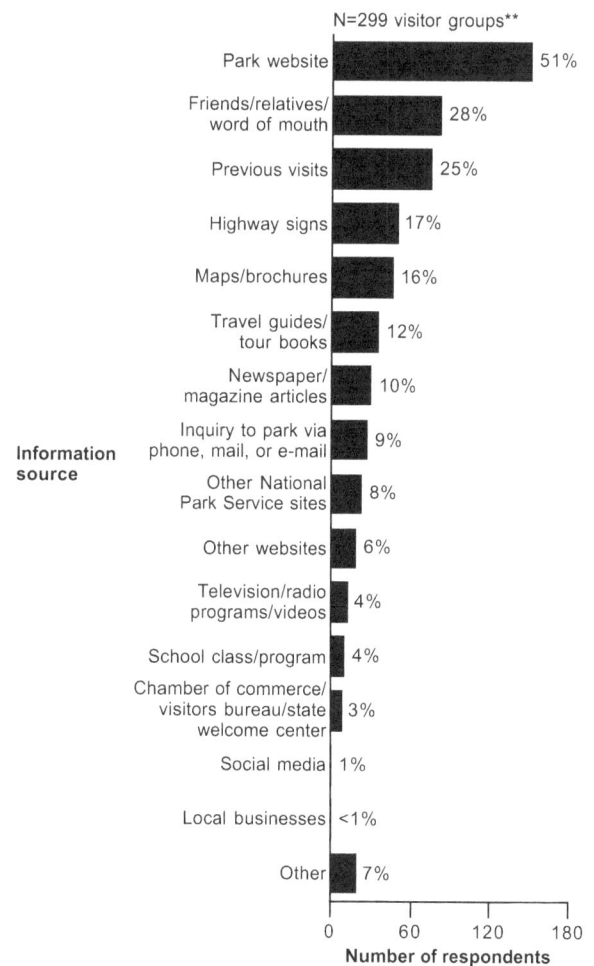

Figure 31. Sources of information

---

*total percentages do not equal 100 due to rounding
**total percentages do not equal 100 because visitors could select more than one answer

Park as destination

Question from on-site interview
A two-minute interview was conducted with each individual selected to complete the questionnaire. During the interview, the question was asked: "How did this visit to Congaree NP fit into your personal group's travel plans?"

Results
- 75% of visitor groups indicated that the park was their primary destination (see Figure 32).

- 23% said the visit to Congaree NP was one of several destinations.

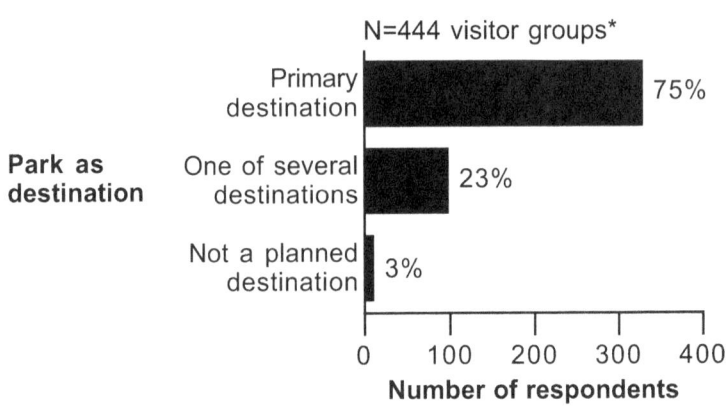

Figure 32. How visit to park fit into visitor groups' travel plans

*total percentages do not equal 100 due to rounding
**total percentages do not equal 100 because visitors could select more than one answer

26

Alternate recreation site

Question 24a

On this trip, if you and your personal group had not chosen to visit Congaree NP, what other recreation site would you have visited instead? (Open-ended)

Results

- 53% of visitor groups (N=173) responded to this question.

- Table 9 lists the places that visitor groups indicated as potential alternate sites they would have visited instead of Congaree NP.

Table 9. Alternate recreation sites
(N=191 comments; some visitors listed more than one site)

Site	Number of times mentioned
None	29
Harbison State Forest	18
Sesquicentennial State Park	7
Other NPS sites	6
Riverbanks Zoo	6
Lake Murray	5
Peachtree Rock	5
Zoo	5
Fort Sumter National Monument	4
River walks - Columbia, SC	4
Santee National Wildlife Refuge	4
State parks	4
Columbia Riverwalk	3
Poinsett State Park	3
Saluda Shoals Park	3
State Museum	3
Fort Sumter National Monument	3
Another park	2
Beidler Forest	2
Caesars Head State Park	2
Francis Marion National Forest	2
Great Smoky Mountains	2
Hot Springs National Park	2
Lake Wateree	2
North Carolina State Park	2
Other comments	63

Question 24b

How far is this alternative site from your home?

Results

- 54% of the visitor groups indicated that they would travel up to 50 miles from their home to visit the alternate site (see Figure 33).

- 33% would travel 151 or more miles.

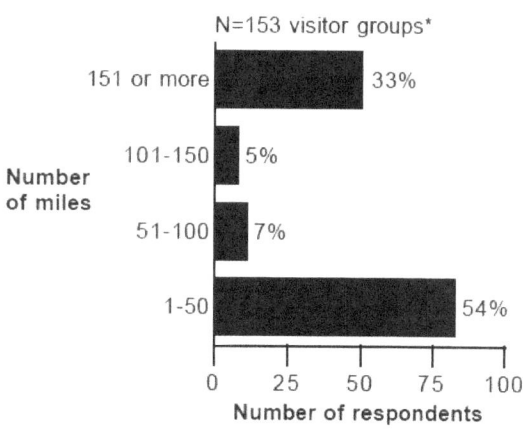

Figure 33. Number of miles to alternate recreation site

---

*total percentages do not equal 100 due to rounding
**total percentages do not equal 100 because visitors could select more than one answer

Primary reason for visiting the park area

Question 7

On this trip, what was the primary reason that you and your personal group came to the Congaree NP area (within 1-hour drive of the park)? '

Results

- 31% of visitor groups were residents of the area within a 1-hour drive of the park (see Figure 34).

- As shown in Figure 35, the most common primary reasons for visiting the area (within a 1-hour drive of the park) among nonresident visitor groups were:

    66% Visit the park
    13% Visit friends/relatives in the area

- "Other" primary reasons (5%) were:

    Attended a conference in Columbia
    Big trees
    Boy Scout Trip
    Camping trip
    Church event
    Columbia, SC Repticon Show
    Hiking
    Limestone College
    Photo opportunities
    Travelling through
    Wetland delineation class

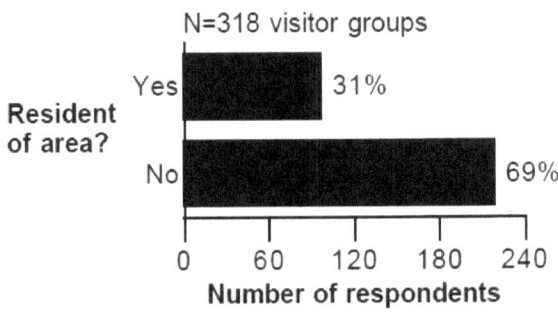

Figure 34. Residents of the area (within a 1-hour drive of the park)

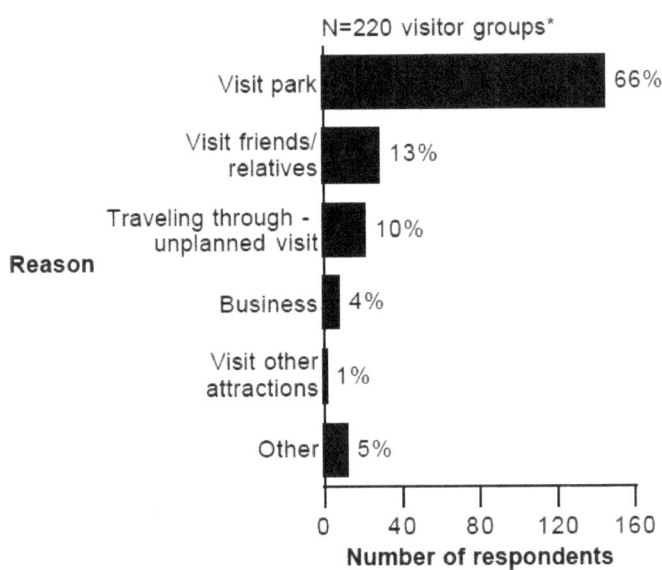

Figure 35. Primary reason for visiting the park area (within a 1-hour drive of the park)

---

*total percentages do not equal 100 due to rounding
**total percentages do not equal 100 because visitors could select more than one answer

Number of vehicles

Question 12

On this visit, how many vehicles did you and your personal group use to arrive at the park?

Results

- 91% of visitor groups used one vehicle to arrive at the park (see Figure 36).

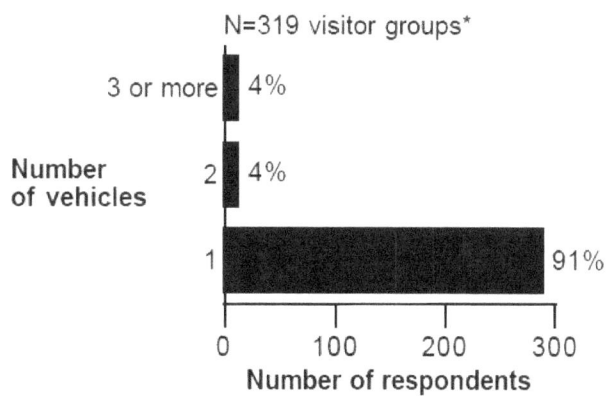

Figure 36. Number of vehicles used to arrive at the park

Overnight stays

Question 9a

On this trip, did you and your personal group stay overnight away from your permanent residence either inside Congaree NP or within the nearby area (within 1-hour drive of the park)?

Results

- 40% of visitor groups stayed overnight away from home either inside the park or the nearby area (see Figure 37).

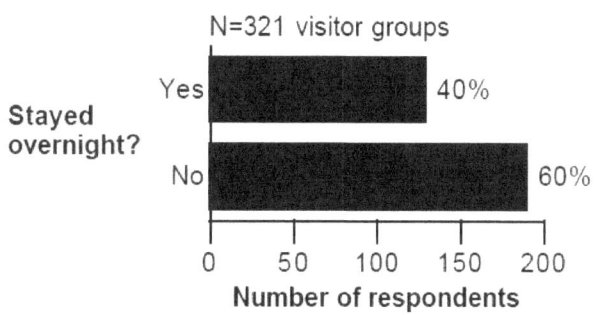

Figure 37. Visitor groups that stayed overnight in the park or within a 1-hour drive of the park

Question 9b

If YES, how many nights did you and your personal group spend inside the park?

Results

- 42% of visitor groups spent one night inside the park (see Figure 38).

- 34% spent two nights.

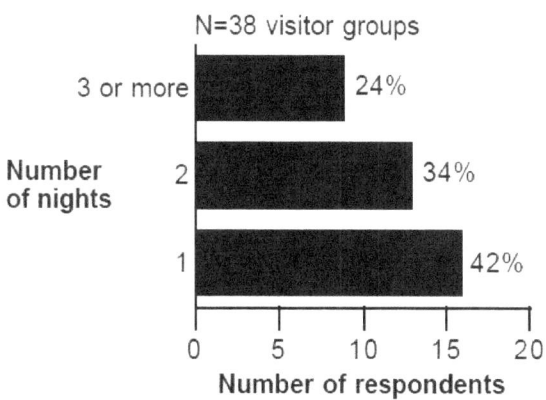

Figure 38. Number of nights spent inside the park

---

*total percentages do not equal 100 due to rounding

**total percentages do not equal 100 because visitors could select more than one answer

Question 9c

If YES, how many nights did you and your personal group spend outside the park within a 1-hour drive?

Results

- 52% of visitor groups stayed one night outside the park within a 1-hour drive of the park (see Figure 39).

- 33% stayed two or three nights.

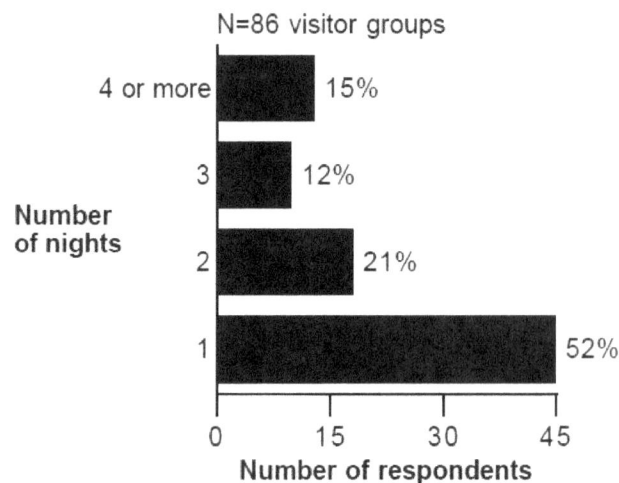

N=86 visitor groups

Figure 39. Number of nights spent in the area outside the park (within a 1-hour drive of the park).

---

*total percentages do not equal 100 due to rounding

**total percentages do not equal 100 because visitors could select more than one answer

Accommodations used inside the park

Question 9b

In which types of accommodations did you and your personal group spend the night(s) inside the park?

Results

* As shown in Figure 40, the most common types of accommodations used inside the park by visitor groups were:

  58% Tent camping
  29% RV/trailer camping

* "Other" type of accommodation (3%) was:

  Van in parking lot

* Table 10 shows the number of nights spent in accommodations inside the park. Accommodations specified by fewer than 30 visitor groups should be interpreted with **CAUTION!**

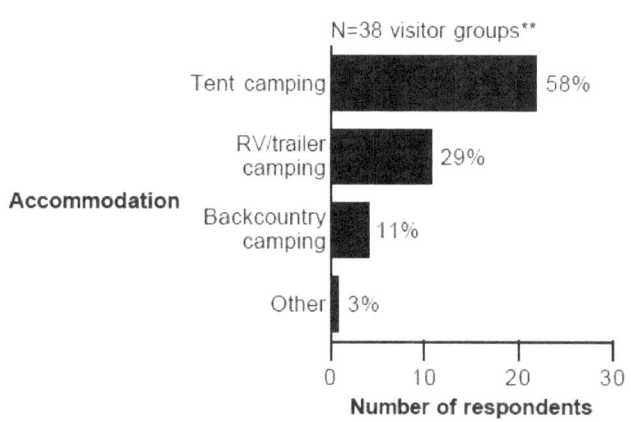

Figure 40. Accommodations used inside the park

Table 10. Number of nights spent in accommodations inside the park – **CAUTION!** (N=number of visitor groups

Accommodation	N	Number of nights (%)*			
		1	2	3	4 or more
Tent camping	22	32	55	14	0
RV/trailer camping	11	45	9	27	18
Backcountry camping	4	100	0	0	0
Other	1	0	0	100	0

*total percentages do not equal 100 due to rounding
**total percentages do not equal 100 because visitors could select more than one answer

Accommodations used outside the park

Question 9c

In which types of accommodations did you and your personal group spend the night(s) outside park within 1-hour drive?

Results

- 71% of visitor groups stayed overnight in a lodge, hotel, motel, cabin, rented condo/home, or bed & breakfast (see Figure 41).

- Table 11 shows the number of nights spent in accommodations outside the park within a 1-hour drive of the park. Accommodations specified by fewer than 30 visitor groups should be interpreted with **CAUTION!**

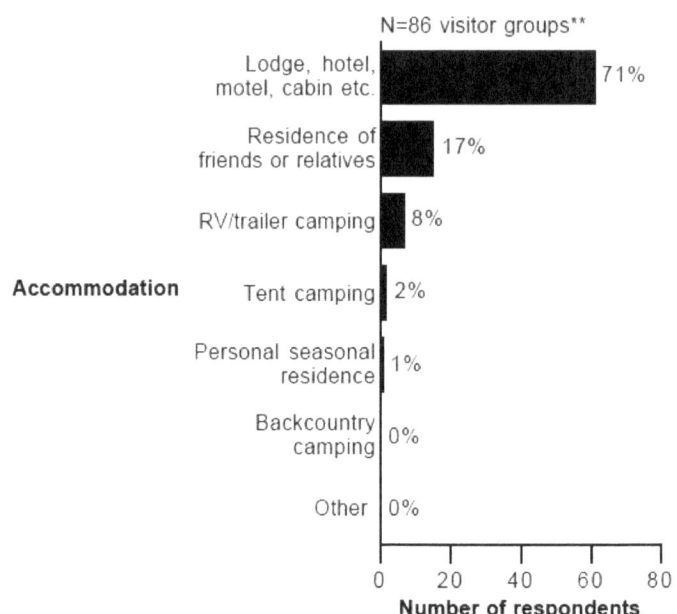

Figure 41. Accommodations used outside the park within a 1-hour drive

Table 11. Number of nights spent in accommodations outside the park within a 1-hour drive (N=number of visitor groups)

Accommodation	N	Number of nights (%) *			
		1	2	3	4 or more
Lodge, hotel, motel, cabin, rented condo/home, or bed & breakfast	61	62	16	11	10
RV/trailer camping – **CAUTION!**	7	14	43	29	14
Tent camping – **CAUTION!**	2	0	100	0	0
Residence of friends or relatives – **CAUTION!**	15	33	20	7	40
Personal seasonal residence – **CAUTION!**	1	100	0	0	0
Backcountry camping – **CAUTION!**	0	0	0	0	0
Other – **CAUTION!**	0	0	0	0	0

*total percentages do not equal 100 due to rounding
**total percentages do not equal 100 because visitors could select more than one answer

Length of stay in the park

Question 13b
On this visit, how long did you and your personal group spend visiting Congaree NP?

Results

Number of hours if less than 24

*   58% spent 3-4 hours in the park (see Figure 42).

*   21% of visitor groups spent 1-2 hours.

*   The average length of stay for visitor groups that spent less than 24 hours was 3.5 hours.

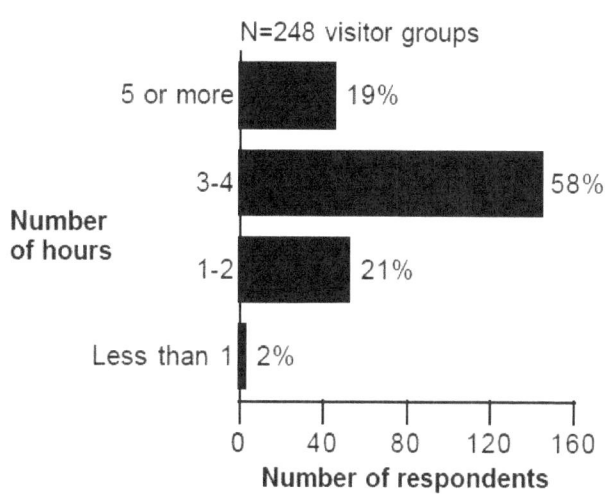

Figure 42. Number of hours spent in the park

Number of days if 24 hours or more

*   58% of visitor groups spent two days in the park (see Figure 43).

*   The average length of stay for visitor groups that spent more than 24 hours was 2.3 days.

Average length of stay for all visitors

*   The average length of stay in the park for all visitor groups was 9.6 hours.

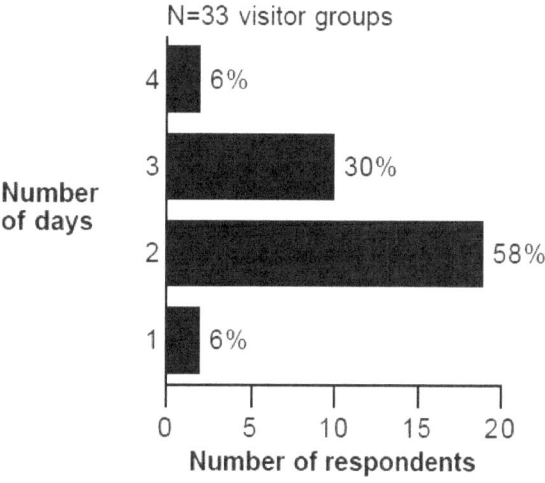

Figure 43. Number of days spent in the park

*total percentages do not equal 100 due to rounding
**total percentages do not equal 100 because visitors could select more than one answer

Length of stay in the park area

Question 13a
How long did you and your personal group stay in the Congaree NP area (within 1-hour drive of the park)?

Results
- 30% of visitor groups were residents of the area within a 1-hour drive of the park (see Figure 44).

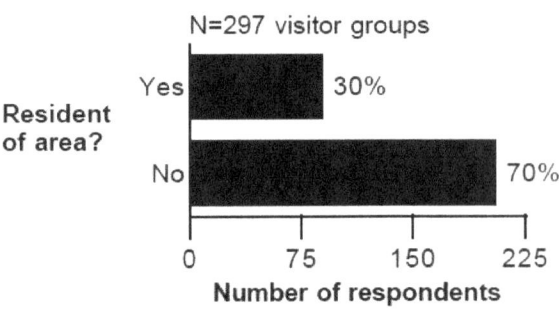

Figure 44. Residents of the area (within 1-hour drive of the park)

Number of hours if less than 24

- 37% of visitor groups spent 3-4 hours in the park area (see Figure 45).

- 24% spent 1-2 hours.

- The average length of stay in the area for visitor groups who spent less than 24 hours was 5.1 hours.

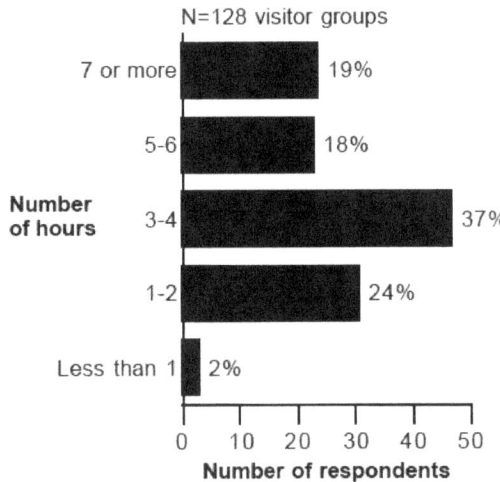

Figure 45. Number of hours spent in the park area (within a 1-hour drive of the park)

Number of days if 24 hours or more

- 54% of visitor groups spent 1-2 days in the park area (see Figure 46).

- 28% spent 3-4 days.

- The average length of stay for visitor groups that spent 24 hours or more was 5.1 days.

Average length of stay for all visitors

- The average length of stay for all visitor groups was 50.0 hours, or 2.1 days.

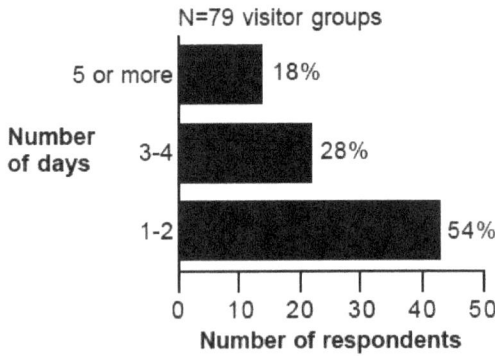

Figure 46. Number of days spent in the park area (within a 1-hour drive of the park)

*total percentages do not equal 100 due to rounding

**total percentages do not equal 100 because visitors could select more than one answer

Sites visited in the Congaree NP area

Question 8
On this visit, which sites did you and your personal group visit in the Congaree NP area (within 1-hour drive of the park)?

- As shown in Figure 47, the sites most commonly visited in the Congaree NP area were:

    20% South Carolina state parks
    19% The State Capitol
    17% University of South Carolina

- The least visited sites were:

    1% Shaw Air Force Base
    1% Harbison State Forest

- "Other" sites (38%) visited are shown in Table 12.

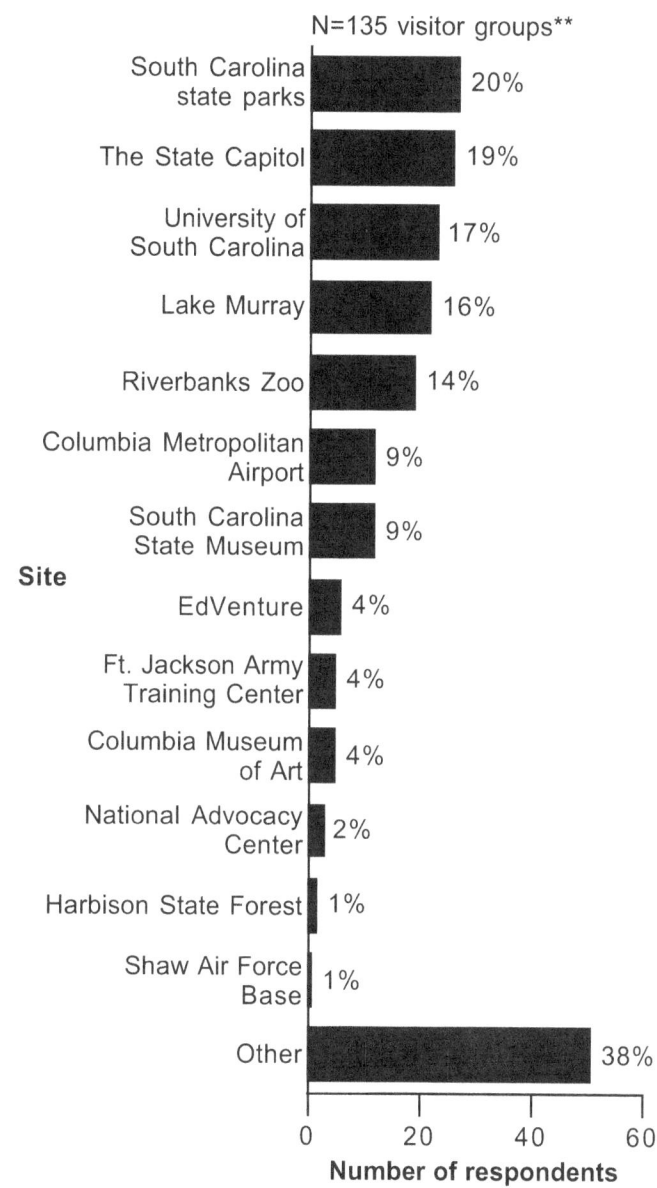

Figure 47. Sites visited in the park area (within a 1-hour drive of the park)

*total percentages do not equal 100 due to rounding

**total percentages do not equal 100 because visitors could select more than one answer

Table 12. "Other" sites visited in the park area
(N=25 comments) – **CAUTION!**

Site	Number of times mentioned
Charleston	3
Santee National Wildlife Refuge	3
Aircraft carrier *Yorktown*	1
Carel Walk	1
City Roots food trucks	1
Civil War Museum in Columbia	1
Columbia airport	1
Columbia Fire Department	1
Congaree River	1
Downtown Columbia	1
Eastover Area	1
Folley Beach	1
Granby Park	1
Hilton Head Island, SC	1
Kensington Mansion	1
Lexington Museum	1
Ninety-Six National Historic Site	1
Richmond County Library	1
Savannah, SC	1
Steeplechase in Camden	1
Three Rivers Walk	1

*total percentages do not equal 100 due to rounding
**total percentages do not equal 100 because visitors could select more than one answer

Activities within the park

Question 11
　　On this visit, in which activities did
　　you and your personal group
　　participate within Congaree NP?

Results
　　• As shown in Figure 48, the most
　　　common activities in which
　　　visitor groups participated were:

　　　　85% Walking/hiking
　　　　74% Visiting the visitor center

　　• "Other" activities (5%) were:

　　　　Enjoying nature
　　　　Enjoy quiet
　　　　Junior Ranger program
　　　　Living history tour
　　　　Movie at visitor center
　　　　Photography
　　　　School event

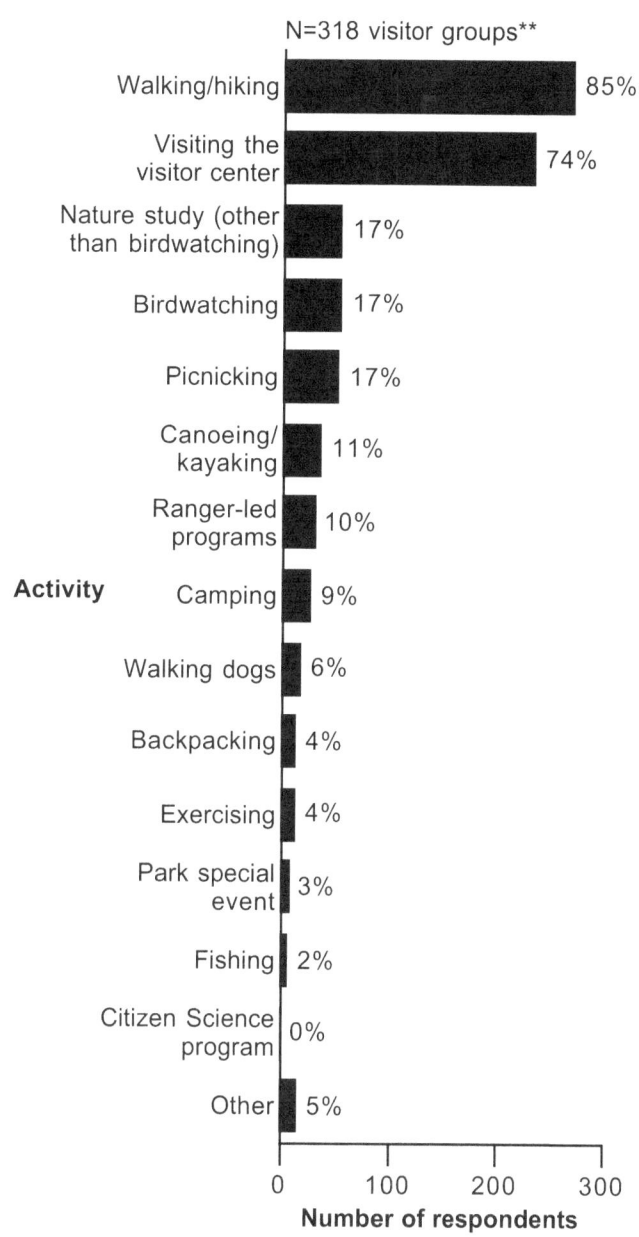

Figure 48. Activities on this visit

---

*total percentages do not equal 100 due to rounding
**total percentages do not equal 100 because visitors could select more than one answer

Use of park trails

Question 10a
On this visit to Congaree NP, did you and your personal group walk/ canoe/kayak any park trails?

Results
- 96% of visitor groups used a park trail in Congaree NP (see Figure 49).

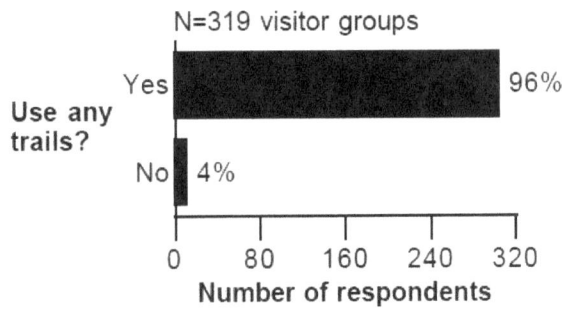

Figure 49. Visitor groups that used park trails

Question 10b
If YES, which of the following trails did you and your personal group walk/ canoe/kayak on this visit?

Results
- As shown in Figure 50, of those visitor groups that used park trails, the most commonly used trails were:

  81% Elevated Boardwalk Trail
  63% Low Boardwalk Trail
  38% Weston Lake Loop Trail

- The least used trail was the Kingsnake Trail (3%).

- Other trails (2%) were:

  Bannister Bridge Canoe Trail
  Dog trails
  From visitor center to campground
  Harry Hampton tree
  Wise Lake

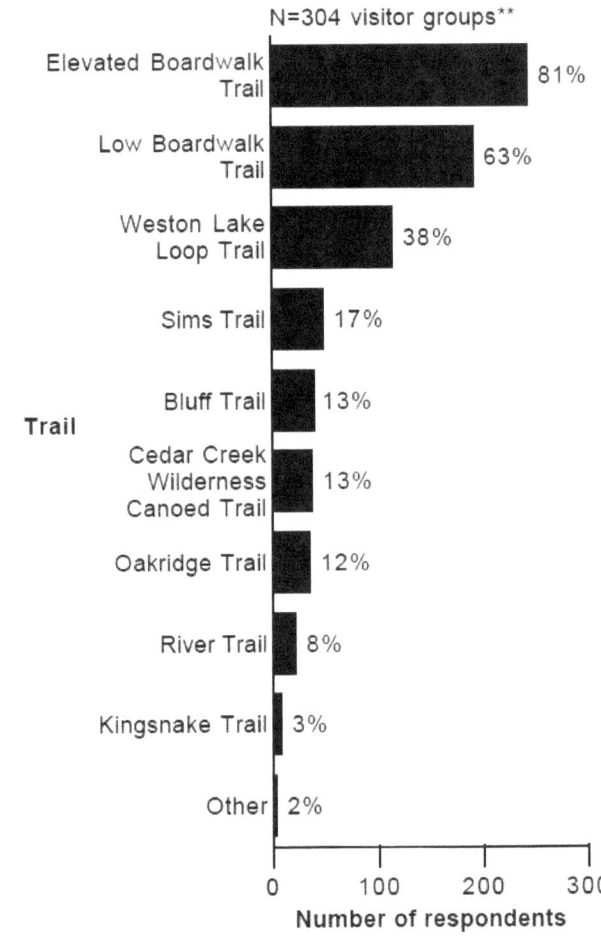

Figure 50. Trails used in Congaree NP

---

*total percentages do not equal 100 due to rounding

**total percentages do not equal 100 because visitors could select more than one answer

Ratings of Services, Facilities, Attributes, Resources, and Elements

Information services and facilities used

Question 16a

Please indicate all of the information services and facilities that you or your personal group used at Congaree NP during this visit.

Results

- As shown in Figure 51, the most common information services and facilities used by visitor groups were:

      87% Park brochure/map
      83% Assistance from park staff
      77% Visitor center exhibits

- The least used service/facility was the Junior Ranger program (6%).

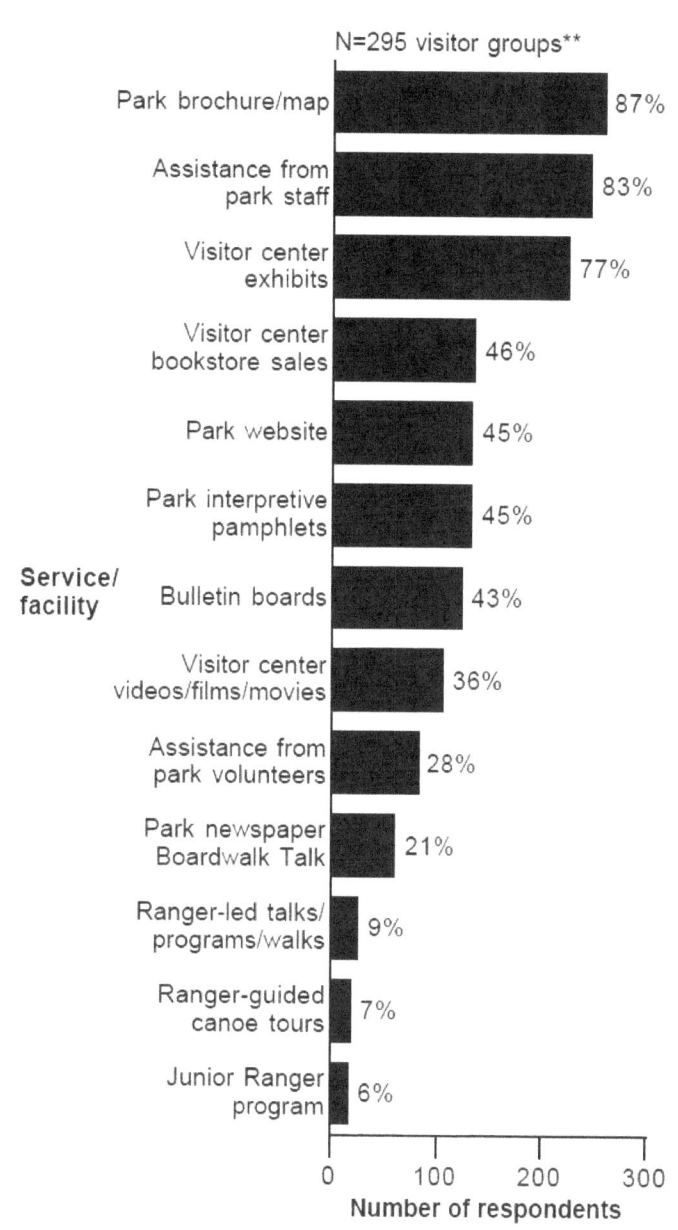

Figure 51. Information services and facilities used

*total percentages do not equal 100 due to rounding

**total percentages do not equal 100 because visitors could select more than one answer

Importance ratings of information services and facilities

Question 16b

For only those services and facilities that you or your personal group used, please rate their importance to your visit from 1-5.

1=Not important
2=Somewhat important
3=Moderately important
4=Very important
5=Extremely important

Results

- Figure 52 shows the combined proportions of "extremely important" and "very important" ratings of information services and facilities that were rated by 30 or more visitor groups.

- The services and facilities receiving the highest combined proportions of "extremely important" and "very important" ratings were:

  93% Park brochure/map
  92% Park website
  84% Assistance from park staff

- Table 13 shows the importance ratings of each service and facility.

- The service/facility receiving the highest "not important" rating that was rated by 30 or more visitor groups was:

  7% Visitor center bookstore sales items

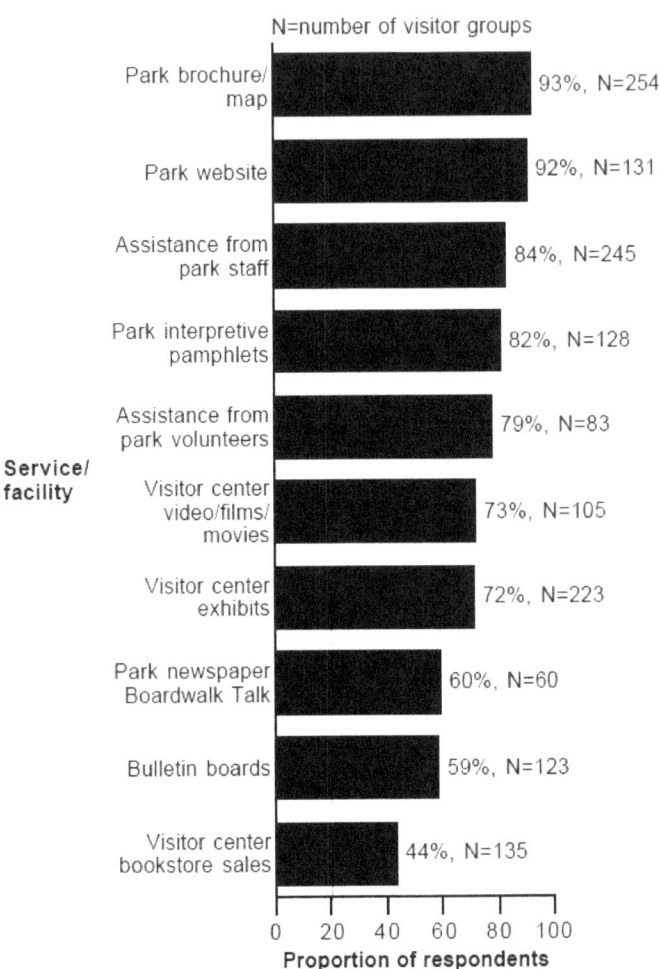

N=number of visitor groups

Figure 52. Combined proportions of "extremely important" and "very important" ratings of information services and facilities

---

*total percentages do not equal 100 due to rounding
**total percentages do not equal 100 because visitors could select more than one answer

Table 13. Importance ratings of information services and facilities
(N=number of visitor groups)

Service/facility	N	Rating (%)*				
		Not important	Somewhat important	Moderately important	Very important	Extremely important
Assistance from park staff	245	1	3	12	42	42
Assistance from park volunteers	83	0	6	16	46	33
Bulletin boards	123	1	11	29	41	18
Junior Ranger program – **CAUTION!**	18	11	0	22	39	28
Park brochure/map	254	0	1	6	35	58
Park interpretive pamphlets	128	2	3	13	41	41
Park newspaper *Boardwalk Talk*	60	5	2	33	43	17
Park website (nps.gov/cong)	131	1	1	7	36	56
Ranger-led talks/programs/walks – **CAUTION!**	28	0	0	7	29	64
Ranger-guided canoe tours – **CAUTION!**	20	0	0	0	20	80
Visitor center bookstore sales items	135	7	15	35	25	19
Visitor center videos/films/movies	105	0	9	18	37	36
Visitor center exhibits	223	0	7	22	39	33

*total percentages do not equal 100 due to rounding
**total percentages do not equal 100 because visitors could select more than one answer

Quality ratings of information services and facilities

Question 16c

For only those services and facilities that you or your personal group used, please rate their quality from 1-5.

      1=Very poor
      2=Poor
      3=Average
      4=Good
      5=Very good

Results

- Figure 53 shows the combined proportions of "very good" and "good" ratings of information services and facilities that were rated by 30 or more visitor groups.

- The services and facilities receiving the highest combined proportions of "very good" and "good" ratings were:

    98% Assistance from park staff
    97% Assistance from park volunteers
    90% Park brochure/map

- Table 14 shows the quality ratings of each service and facility.

- The services/facilities receiving the highest "not important" ratings that were rated by 30 or more visitor groups were:

    1% Assistance from park volunteers
    1% Park website

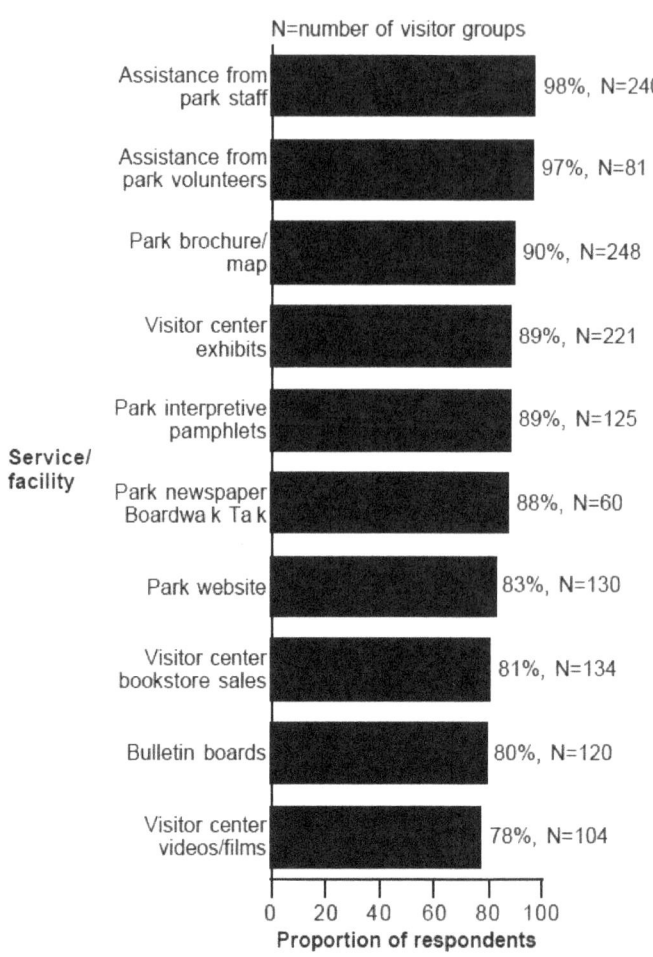

Figure 53. Combined proportions of "very good" and "good" ratings of information services and facilities

---

*total percentages do not equal 100 due to rounding

**total percentages do not equal 100 because visitors could select more than one answer

Table 14. Quality ratings of information services and facilities
(N=number of visitor groups)

Service/facility	N	Rating (%)*				
		Very Poor	Poor	Average	Good	Very good
Assistance from park staff	240	0	1	1	13	85
Assistance from park volunteers	81	1	0	1	22	75
Bulletin boards	120	0	2	18	41	39
Junior Ranger program – **CAUTION!**	16	0	0	0	44	56
Park brochure/map	248	0	1	9	32	58
Park interpretive pamphlets	125	0	2	8	35	54
Park newspaper *Boardwalk Talk*	60	0	2	10	45	43
Park website (nps.gov/cong)	130	1	2	15	40	43
Ranger-led talks/ programs/walks – **CAUTION!**	28	0	0	4	14	82
Ranger-guided canoe tours – **CAUTION!**	20	0	0	0	25	75
Visitor center bookstore sales items	134	0	1	19	36	45
Visitor center videos/films/movies	104	0	2	20	38	40
Visitor center exhibits	221	0	2	9	34	55

*total percentages do not equal 100 due to rounding

**total percentages do not equal 100 because visitors could select more than one answer

Mean scores of importance and quality ratings of information services and facilities

- Figures 54 and 55 show the mean scores of importance and quality ratings of information and facilities that were rated by 30 or more visitor groups.

- All information services and facilities were rated above average.

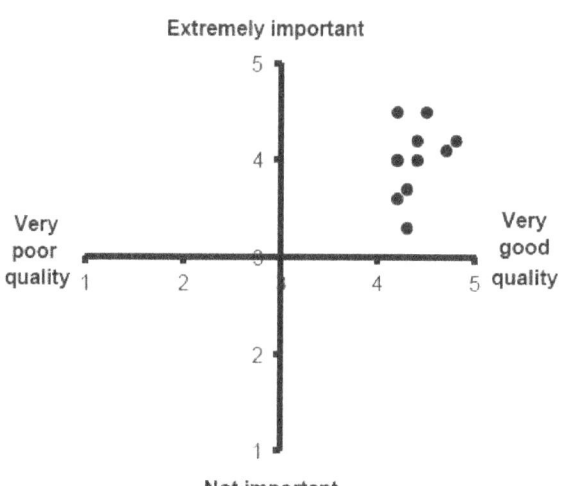

Figure 54. Mean scores of importance and quality ratings of information services and facilities

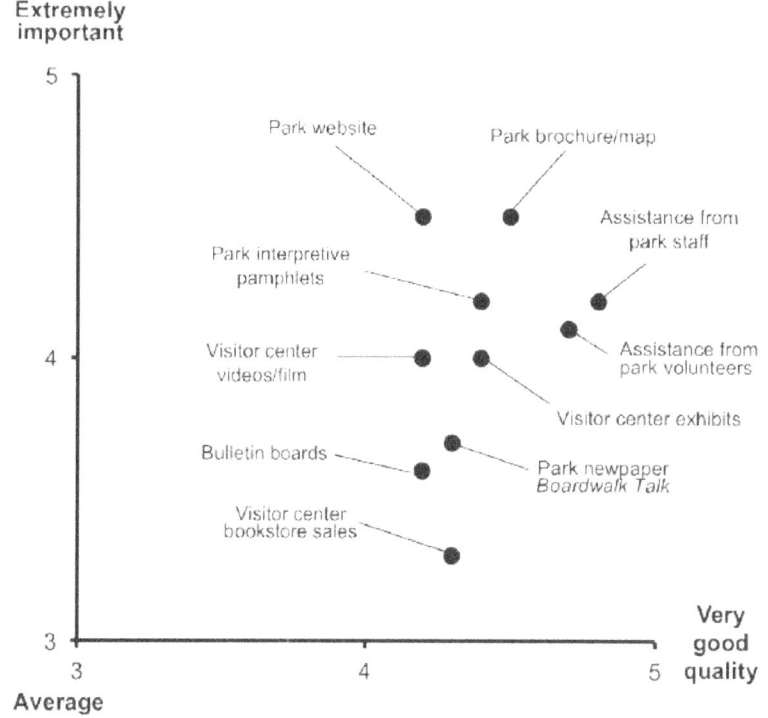

Figure 55. Detail of Figure 54

---

*total percentages do not equal 100 due to rounding

**total percentages do not equal 100 because visitors could select more than one answer

Visitor services and facilities used

Question 17a
Please indicate all of the
visitor services and facilities
that you or your personal
group used at Congaree NP
during this visit.

Results
- As shown in Figure 56,
  the most common visitor
  services and facilities
  used by visitor groups
  were:

  91% Boardwalks
  90% Restrooms
  88% Parking areas

- The least used service/
  facility was:

  4% Backcountry camping

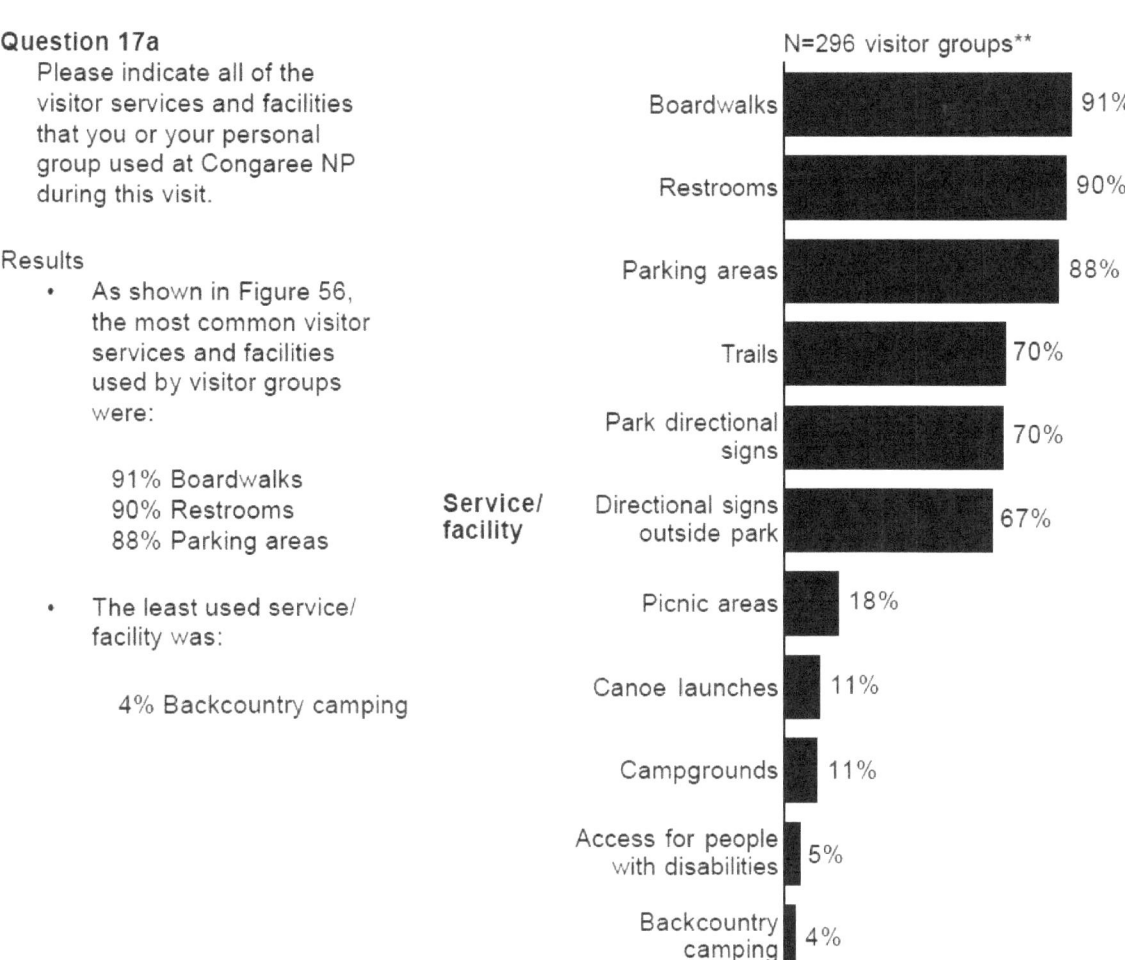

N=296 visitor groups**

**Service/
facility**

Figure 56. Visitor services and facilities used

---

*total percentages do not equal 100 due to rounding
**total percentages do not equal 100 because visitors could select more than one answer

Importance ratings of visitor services and facilities

Question 17b

For only those services and facilities that you or your personal group used, please rate their importance to your visit from 1-5.

1=Not important
2=Somewhat important
3=Moderately important
4=Very important
5=Extremely important

Results

- Figure 57 shows the combined proportions of "extremely important" and "very important" ratings of visitor services and facilities that were rated by 30 or more visitor groups.

- The visitor services and facilities receiving the highest combined proportions of "extremely important" and "very important" ratings were:

   99% Trails
   94% Restrooms
   94% Campgrounds

- Table 16 shows the importance ratings of each service and facility.

- The service/facility receiving the highest "not important" rating that was rated by 30 or more visitor groups was:

   1% Parking areas

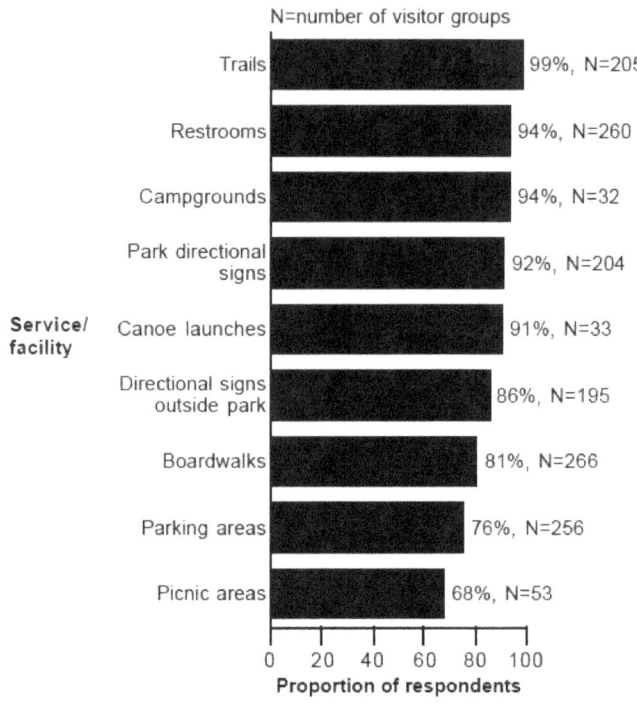

N=number of visitor groups

Figure 57. Combined proportions of "extremely important" and "very important" ratings of visitor services and facilities

---

*total percentages do not equal 100 due to rounding

**total percentages do not equal 100 because visitors could select more than one answer

Table 16. Importance ratings of visitor services and facilities
(N=number of visitor groups)

Service/facility	N	Rating (%)*				
		Not important	Somewhat important	Moderately important	Very important	Extremely important
Access for people with disabilities – **CAUTION!**	14	0	14	7	21	57
Backcountry camping – **CAUTION!**	12	0	0	0	17	83
Boardwalks	266	<1	3	16	28	53
Campgrounds	32	0	0	6	41	53
Canoe launches	33	0	0	9	30	61
Directional signs outside of park	195	0	3	11	34	52
Park directional signs	204	0	2	5	31	61
Parking areas	256	1	3	20	35	41
Picnic areas	53	0	4	28	38	30
Restrooms	260	0	1	5	27	67
Trails	205	0	0	<1	19	80

*total percentages do not equal 100 due to rounding

**total percentages do not equal 100 because visitors could select more than one answer

Quality ratings of visitor services and facilities

Question 17c
For only those services and facilities that you or your personal group used, please rate their quality from 1-5.

1=Very poor
2=Poor
3=Average
4=Good
5=Very good

Results
- Figure 58 shows the combined proportions of "very good" and "good" ratings of visitor services and facilities that were rated by 30 or more visitor groups.

- The services and facilities receiving the highest combined proportions of "very good" and "good" ratings were:

    96% Trails
    96% Boardwalks
    95% Restrooms

- Table 17 shows the quality ratings of each service and facility.

- The services/facilities receiving the highest "very poor" ratings that were rated by 30 or more visitor groups were:

    3% Canoe launches
    3% Campgrounds

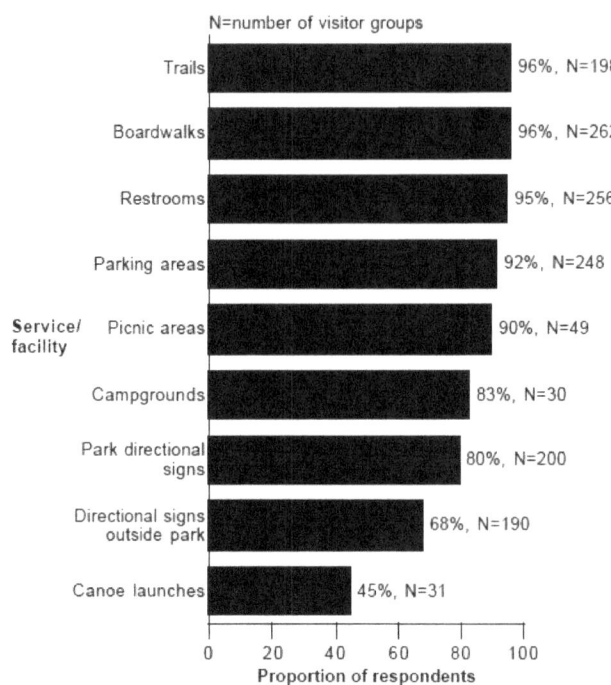

N=number of visitor groups

Figure 58. Combined proportions of "very good" and "good" ratings of visitor services and facilities

*total percentages do not equal 100 due to rounding
**total percentages do not equal 100 because visitors could select more than one answer

Table 17. Quality ratings of visitor services and facilities
(N=number of visitor groups)

Service/facility	N	Rating (%)*				
		Very poor	Poor	Average	Good	Very good
Access for people with disabilities – **CAUTION!**	14	0	7	0	36	57
Backcountry camping – **CAUTION!**	11	0	0	18	27	55
Boardwalks	262	0	0	4	21	75
Campgrounds	30	3	3	10	43	40
Canoe launches	31	3	23	29	26	19
Directional signs outside of park	190	1	8	23	28	40
Park directional signs	200	0	3	18	34	46
Parking areas	248	1	0	7	31	61
Picnic areas	49	0	0	10	39	51
Restrooms	256	<1	1	3	22	73
Trails	198	0	1	4	26	70

*total percentages do not equal 100 due to rounding
**total percentages do not equal 100 because visitors could select more than one answer

Mean scores of importance and quality ratings of visitor services and facilities

- Figures 59 and 60 show the mean scores of importance and quality ratings of visitor services and facilities that were rated by 30 or more visitor groups.

- All visitor services and facilities were rated above average.

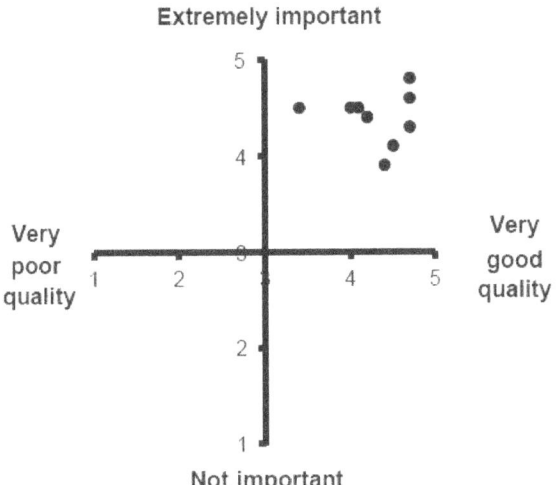

Figure 59. Mean scores of importance and quality of visitor services and facilities

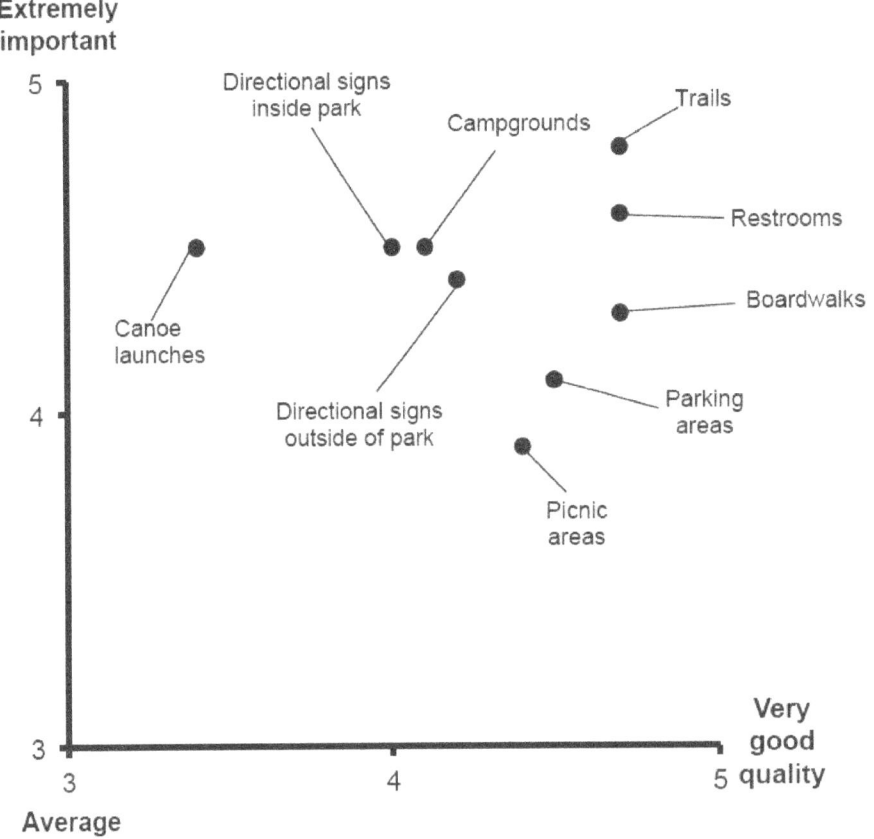

Figure 60. Detail of Figure 59

---

*total percentages do not equal 100 due to rounding

**total percentages do not equal 100 because visitors could select more than one answer

Importance of protecting park resources and attributes

Question 14

It is the National Park Service's responsibility to protect Congaree NP's natural, scenic, and cultural resources while at the same time providing for public enjoyment. How important is protection of the following resources/attributes in the park to you and your personal group?

    1=Not important
    2=Somewhat important
    3=Moderately important
    4=Very important
    5=Extremely important

Results

- As shown in Figure 61, the highest combined proportions of "extremely important" and "very important" ratings of protecting park resources and attributes included:

    94% Clean water
    93% Clean air (visibility)
    92% Natural quiet/sounds of nature

- Table 18 shows the importance ratings of each resource/attribute.

- The resource/attribute receiving the highest "not important" rating was:

    8% Clear night sky (stargazing)

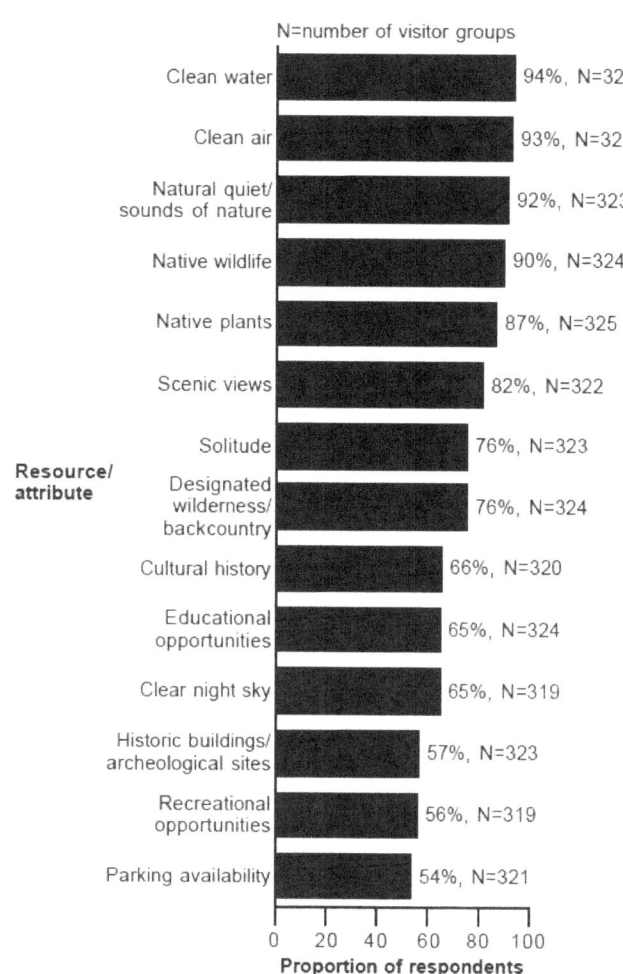

Figure 61. Combined proportions of "extremely important" and "very important" ratings of protecting park resources and attributes

---

*total percentages do not equal 100 due to rounding
**total percentages do not equal 100 because visitors could select more than one answer

Table 18. Importance of protecting park resources and attributes
(N=number of visitor groups)

Resource/attribute	N	Rating (%)*				
		Not important	Somewhat important	Moderately important	Very important	Extremely important
Clean air (visibility)	325	1	1	5	35	58
Clean water	323	1	1	5	29	65
Clear night sky (star gazing)	319	8	8	19	34	31
Cultural history (photographs/artifacts/oral histories)	320	1	8	25	38	28
Designated wilderness/ backcountry	324	2	5	16	30	46
Educational opportunities	324	2	7	26	38	27
Historic buildings/ archeological sites	323	2	10	30	33	24
Native plants	325	1	2	10	35	52
Native wildlife	324	1	2	7	34	56
Natural quiet/sounds of nature	323	1	2	5	30	62
Parking availability	321	2	12	31	34	20
Recreational opportunities	319	3	13	29	36	20
Scenic views	322	2	3	13	39	43
Solitude	323	2	4	18	35	41

*total percentages do not equal 100 due to rounding
**total percentages do not equal 100 because visitors could select more than one answer

Elements that affected park experience

Question 29

Please indicate how the following elements may have affected you and your personal group's park experience during this visit to Congaree NP?

Results

- Most elements had no effect on visitors' experience (see Table 19).

- The elements that most added to visitors' experiences were:

  38% Small numbers of visitors on trails
  29% Small numbers of visitors canoeing/kayaking

- The elements that most detracted from visitors' experiences were:

  42% Airplane noises
  34% Gunshots from neighboring lands

- "Other" elements that added to visitors' experiences (43%) included:

  Beautiful weather
  Clean/absence of litter
  Interpretive steps on boardwalk
  Peaceful sounds
  Quality of visitor center
  Quiet
  Rangers
  Trail for dog
  Wildlife

- "Other" elements that detracted from visitors' experiences (29%) included:

  Cub Scouts
  Dogs and runners on boardwalk
  Inability to rent canoes
  Lack of access/distance to fishing
  Lack of historical markers
  Loud children
  Need a better distinction of what was old growth
  Rainy weather
  Wide, road-like trails

---

*total percentages do not equal 100 due to rounding
**total percentages do not equal 100 because visitors could select more than one answer

Table 19. Effects of different elements on the park experience
(N=total number of visitor groups that responded to the question)
n_1 = number of visitor groups that rated each element
n_2 = number of visitor groups that did not experience each element)

Element	Total N	Rating (%)*				Did not experience	
		n_1	Detracted from	No effect	Added to	n_2	% of total
Airplane noise	313	126	42	57	1	187	60
Automobile noise	315	104	13	87	0	211	67
Gunshots from neighboring lands	316	79	34	61	5	237	75
Noise from park staff activities	316	74	18	82	0	242	77
Train noise	315	60	7	83	1	255	81
Other visitors' activities	311	243	15	77	9	68	22
Small number of visitors on trails	315	280	3	59	38	35	11
Large number of visitors on trails	310	109	32	62	6	201	65
Small number of visitors canoeing/kayaking	314	70	1	70	29	244	78
Large number of visitors canoeing/kayaking	314	45	22	73	4	269	86
Impact of wild pigs	316	85	25	51	25	231	73
Other	95	35	29	29	43	60	63

*total percentages do not equal 100 due to rounding

**total percentages do not equal 100 because visitors could select more than one answer

Expenditures

Total expenditures inside and outside the park

Question 26

For you and your personal group, please estimate all expenditures for the items listed below for this visit to Congaree NP and the surrounding area (within 1-hour drive of the park).

Results

- 69% of visitor groups spent $1-$200 (see Figure 62).

- 12% spent $201-$400.

- The average visitor group expenditure was $181.

- The median group expenditure (50% of groups spent more and 50% of groups spent less) was $52.

- The average total expenditure per person (per capita) was $75.

- As shown in Figure 63, the largest proportions of total expenditures inside and outside the park were:

  31% Lodges, hotels, motels, cabins, B&B, etc.
  22% Gas and oil
  18% Restaurants and bars

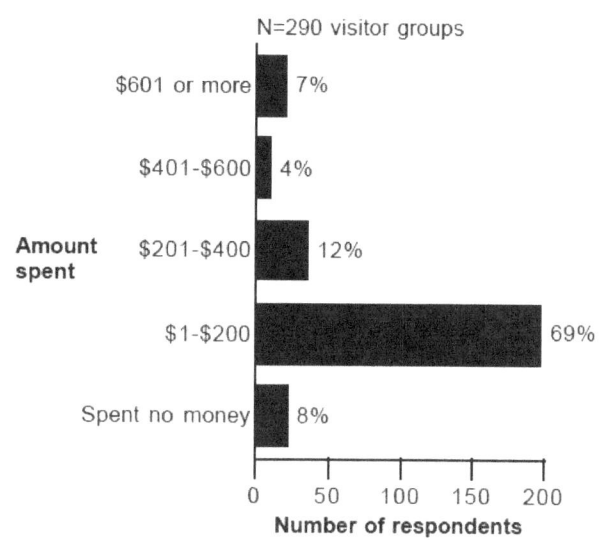

Figure 62. Total expenditures inside and outside the park within a 1-hour drive

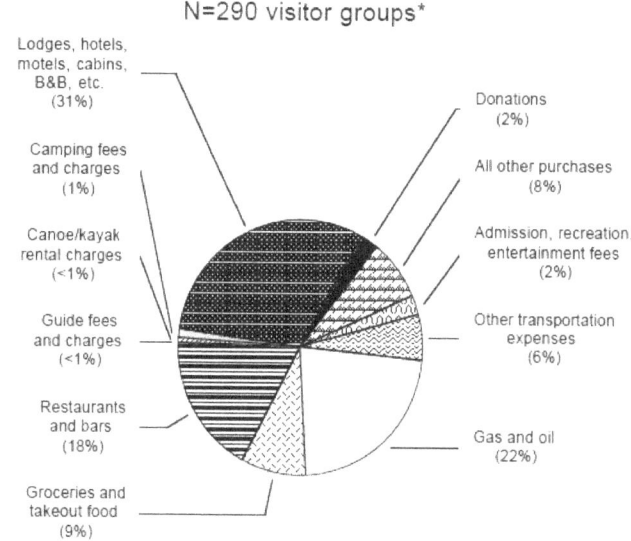

Figure 63. Proportions of total expenditures inside and outside the park within a 1-hour drive

---

*total percentages do not equal 100 due to rounding

**total percentages do not equal 100 because visitors could select more than one answer

Number of children covered by expenditures

Question 26c
How many adults (18 years or older) do
these expenses cover?

Results
- 58% of visitor groups had two
  adults covered by expenditures
  (see Figure 64).

- 21% had one adult covered by
  expenditures.

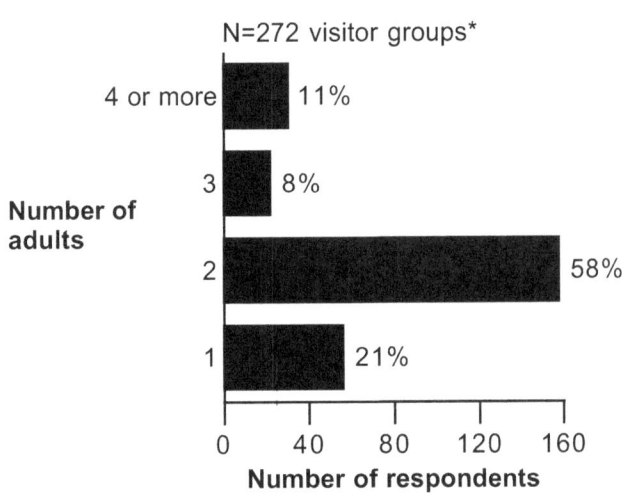

Figure 64. Number of adults covered by
expenditures

Number of children covered by expenditures

Question 26c
How many children (under 18 years) do
these expenses cover?

Results
- 73% of visitor groups had no
  children covered by expenditures
  (see Figure 65).

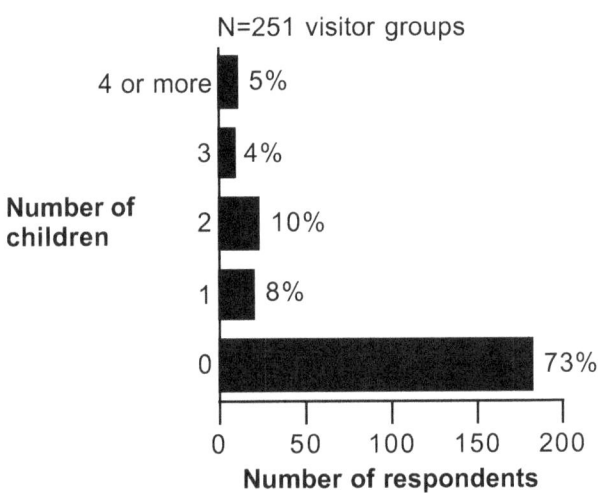

Figure 65. Number of children covered by
expenditures

---

*total percentages do not equal 100 due to rounding
**total percentages do not equal 100 because visitors could select more than one answer

Expenditures inside the park

Question 26a
Please list your personal group's total expenditures inside Congaree NP.

Results

- 46% of visitor groups spent $1-$25 (see Figure 66).

- 41% spent no money inside the park.

- The average visitor group expenditure inside the park was $14.

- The median group expenditure (50% of groups spent more and 50% of groups spent less) was $6.

- The average total expenditure per person (per capita) was $10.

- As shown in Figure 67, the largest proportion of total expenditures inside the park was:

  82% All other purchases

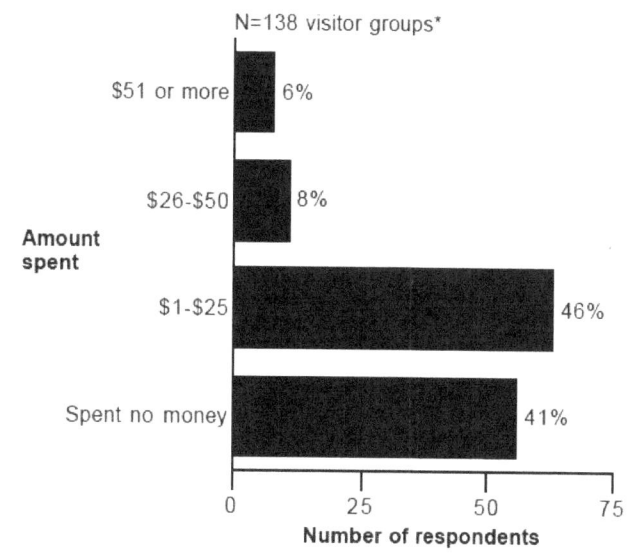

Figure 66. Total expenditures inside the park

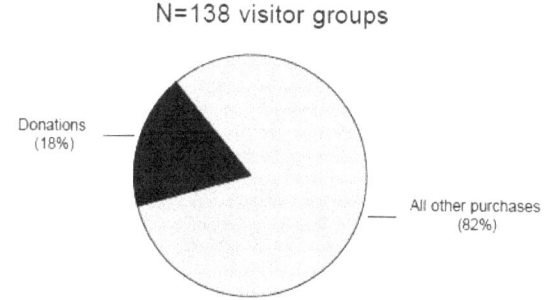

Figure 67. Proportions of total expenditures inside the park

*total percentages do not equal 100 due to rounding
**total percentages do not equal 100 because visitors could select more than one answer

All other purchases (souvenirs, film, books, sporting goods, clothing, etc.)

- 45% of visitor groups spent no money on other purchases inside the park (see Figure 68).

- 19% spent $1-$10.

- 19% spent $21 or more.

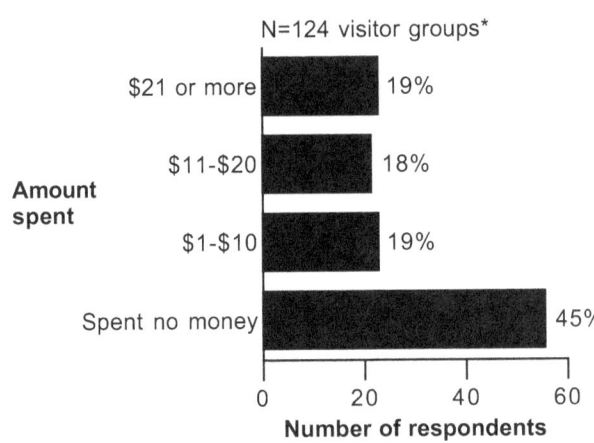

Figure 68. Expenditures for all other purchases inside the park

Donations

- 78% of visitor groups spent no money on donations inside the park (see Figure 69).

- 13% spent $1-$5.

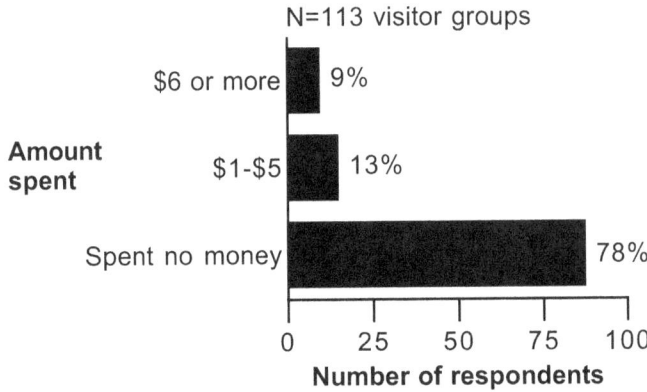

Figure 69. Expenditures for donations inside the park

---

*total percentages do not equal 100 due to rounding
**total percentages do not equal 100 because visitors could select more than one answer

Expenditures outside the park

Question 26b

Please list your personal group's total expenditures in the surrounding area outside the park (within 1-hour drive of park).

Results

- 65% of visitor groups spent $1-$200 (see Figure 70).

- 13% spent $201-$400.

- The average visitor group expenditure outside the park was $183.

- The median group expenditure (50% of groups spent more and 50% of groups spent less) was $50.

- The average total expenditure per person (per capita) was $81.

- As shown in Figure 71, the largest proportions of total expenditures outside the park were:

    32% Lodges, hotels, motels, cabins, B&B, etc.
    23% Gas and oil
    19% Restaurants and bars

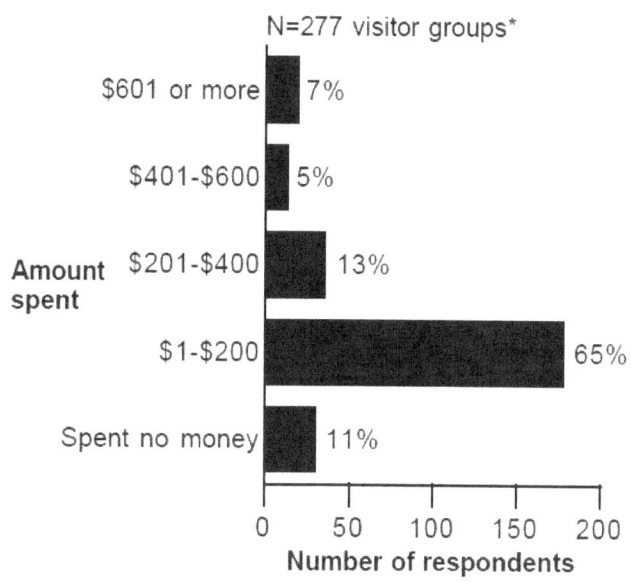

Figure 70. Total expenditures outside the park within a 1-hour drive

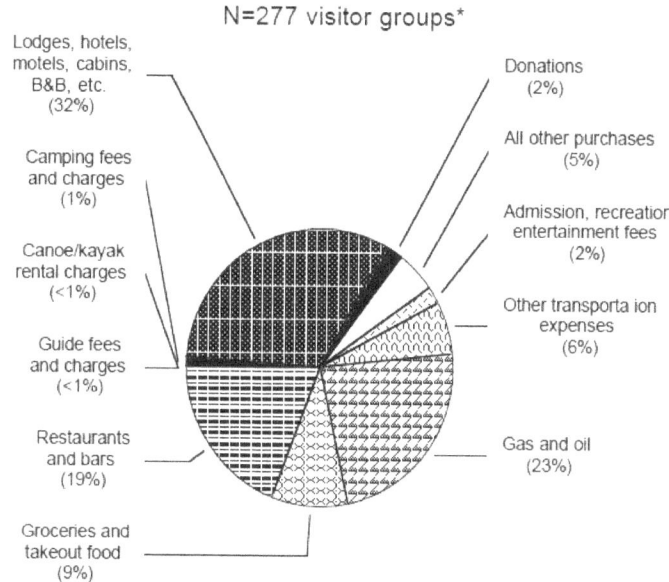

Figure 71. Proportions of total expenditures outside the park within a 1-hour drive

---

*total percentages do not equal 100 due to rounding

**total percentages do not equal 100 because visitors could select more than one answer

Lodges, hotels, motels, cabins, B&B, etc.

- 68% of visitor groups spent no money on lodging outside the park (see Figure 72).

- 13% spent $1-$100.

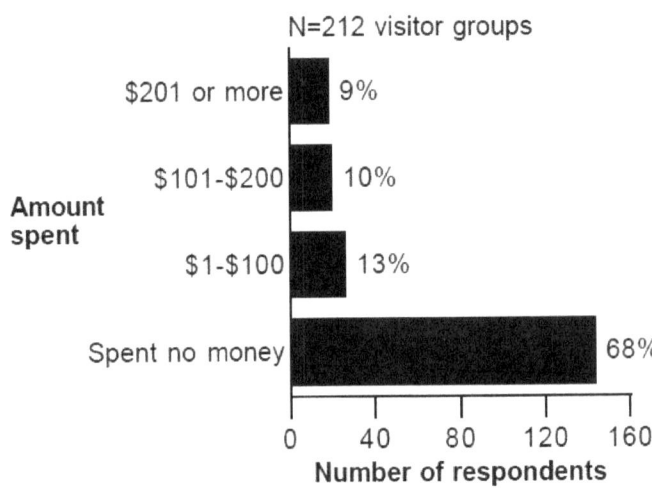

N=212 visitor groups

Figure 72. Expenditures for lodging outside the park

Camping fees and charges

- 92% of visitor groups spent no money on camping fees and charges outside the park (see Figure 73).

- 6% spent $1-$50.

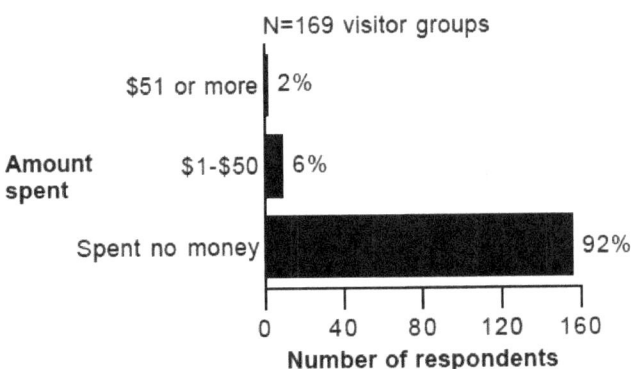

N=169 visitor groups

Figure 73. Expenditures for camping fees and charges outside the park

*total percentages do not equal 100 due to rounding
**total percentages do not equal 100 because visitors could select more than one answer

60

Canoe/kayak rental charges

- 99% of visitor groups spent no money on canoe/kayak rental charges outside the park (see Figure 74).

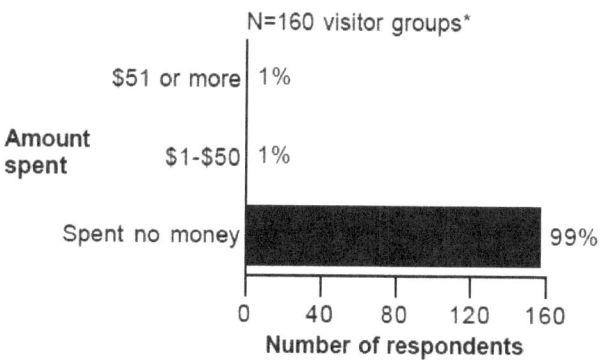

Figure 74. Expenditures for canoe/kayak rental charges outside the park

Guide fees and charges

- 99% of visitor groups spent no money on guide fees and charges outside the park (see Figure 75).

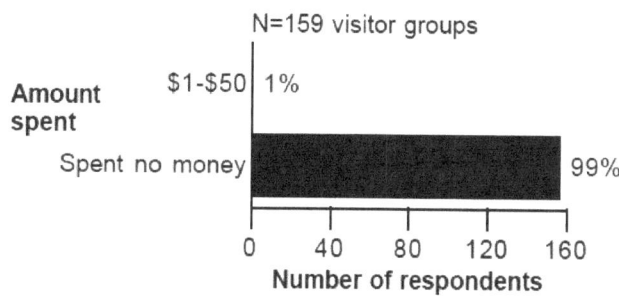

Figure 75. Expenditures for guide fees and charges outside the park

Restaurants and bars

- 45% of visitor groups spent no money on restaurants and bars outside the park (see Figure 76).

- 35% spent $1-$50.

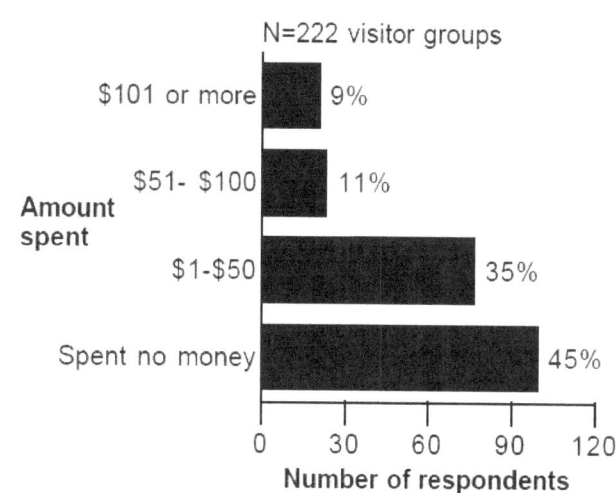

Figure 76. Expenditures for restaurants and bars outside the park

---

*total percentages do not equal 100 due to rounding

**total percentages do not equal 100 because visitors could select more than one answer

Groceries and takeout food

- 53% of visitor groups spent no money on groceries and takeout food outside the park (see Figure 77).

- 37% spent $1-$50.

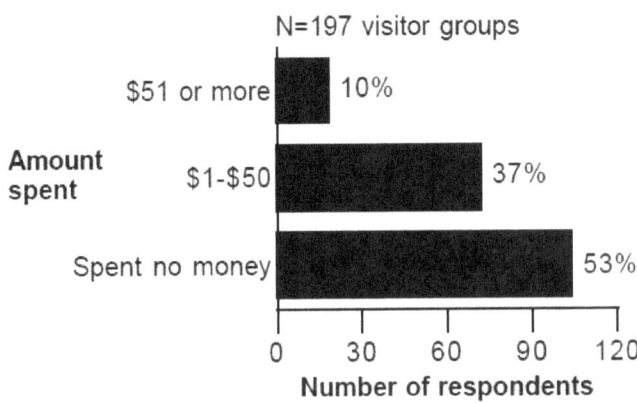

Figure 77. Expenditures for groceries and takeout food outside the park

Gas and oil (auto, RV, boat, etc.)

- 63% of visitor groups spent $1-$50 on gas and oil outside the park (see Figure 78).

- 15% spent $51-$100.

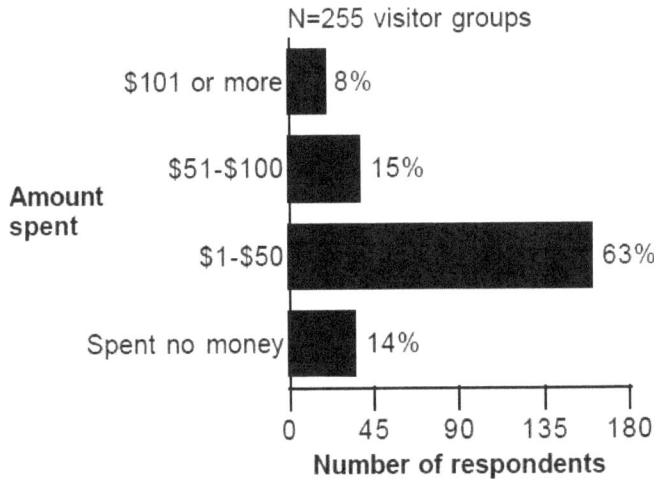

Figure 78. Expenditures for gas and oil outside the park

---

*total percentages do not equal 100 due to rounding

**total percentages do not equal 100 because visitors could select more than one answer

Other transportation (rental cars, taxis, auto repairs, but NOT airfare)

- 90% of visitor groups spent no money on other transportation outside the park (see Figure 79).

- 7% spent $51 or more.

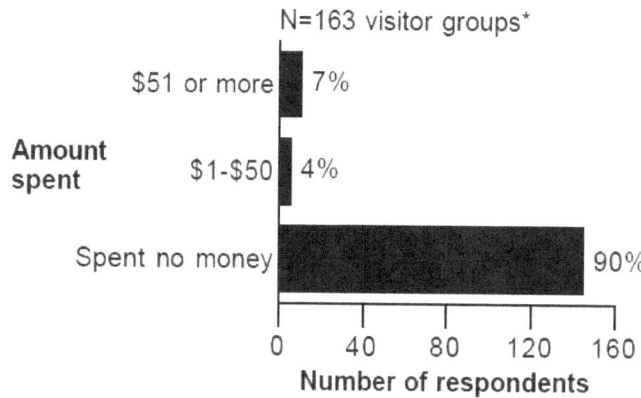

Figure 79. Expenditures for other transportation outside the park

Admission, recreation and entertainment fees

- 90% of visitor groups spent no money on admission, recreation and entertainment fees outside the park (see Figure 80).

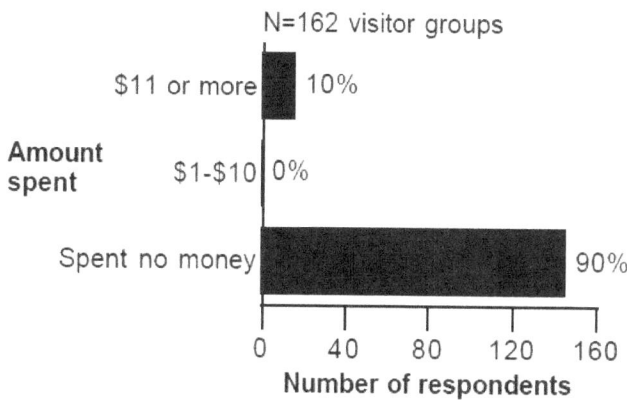

Figure 80. Expenditures for admission, recreation, and entertainment fees outside the park

---

*total percentages do not equal 100 due to rounding

**total percentages do not equal 100 because visitors could select more than one answer

<u>All other purchases</u> (souvenirs, film, books, sporting goods, clothing, etc.)

- 71% of visitor groups spent no money on all other purchases outside the park (see Figure 81).

- 25% spent $1-$50.

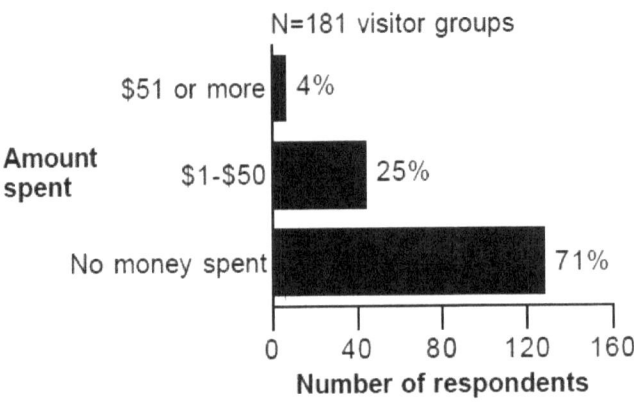

Figure 81. Expenditures for all other purchases outside the park

<u>Donations</u>

- 91% of visitor groups spent no money on donations outside the park (see Figure 82).

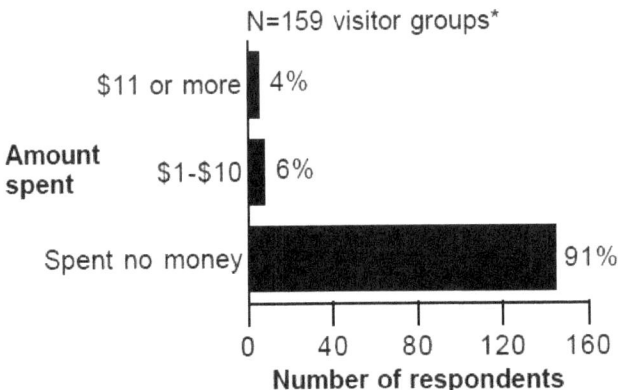

Figure 82. Expenditures for donations outside the park

Unpaid vacation/unpaid time off

Question 25c
Did your household take any unpaid vacation or take unpaid time off of work to come on this trip?

Results
- 13% of visitor groups took unpaid vacation or unpaid time off work to come on this trip (see Figure 83).

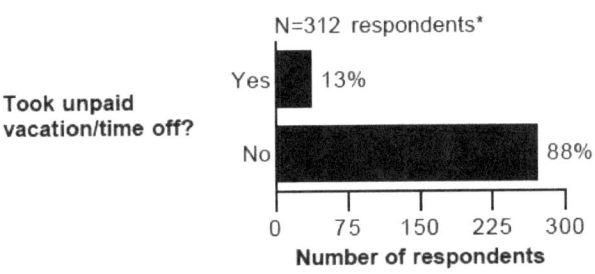

Figure 83. Respondents that took unpaid vacation/ time off to come on this trip

---

*total percentages do not equal 100 due to rounding
**total percentages do not equal 100 because visitors could select more than one answer

Preferences for Future Visits

Likelihood of future visit

Question 28

Would you and your group be likely to visit Congaree NP again in the future?

Results

- 80% of visitor groups indicated that they would be likely to visit Congaree again in the future (see Figure 84).

- 15% were not sure about visiting the park in the future.

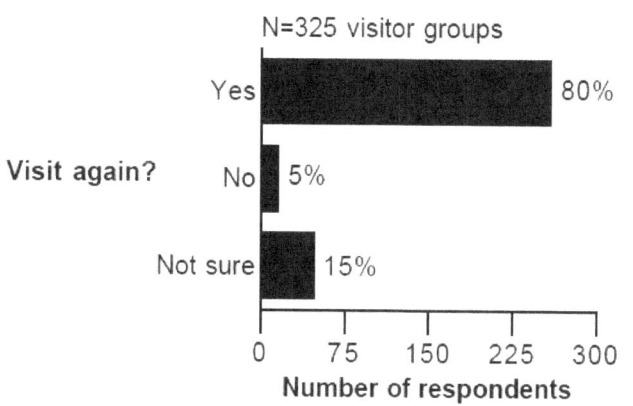

Figure 84. Visitor groups that would likely visit Congaree NP in the future

*total percentages do not equal 100 due to rounding
**total percentages do not equal 100 because visitors could select more than one answer

65

Preferred activities and programs on future visits

Question 30
If you were to visit Congaree NP in the future, which types of organized activities and programs would you and your personal group like to have available?

Results
- 81% of visitor groups were interested in attending organized activities or programs on a future visit to the park (see Figure 85).

- As shown in Figure 86, of those visitor groups that wanted organized activities/programs, the most preferred were:

  65% Canoeing/kayaking
  57% Night walk/night sky program
  53% Owl prowls

- "Other" activities/programs (4%) were:

  Archaeological tours
  Backpacking
  Camping
  Canoe rentals
  Ecology-based workshop
  Entomology education
  Horseback riding
  Nature walks

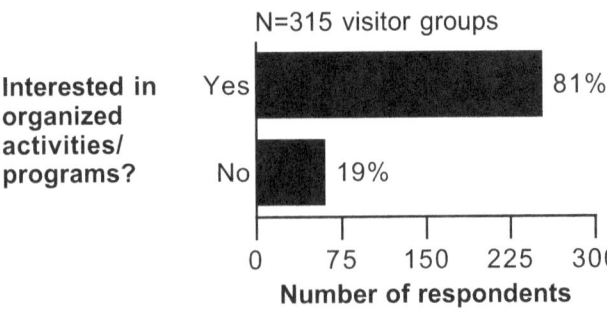

Interested in organized activities/ programs?

N=315 visitor groups

Figure 85. Visitor groups interested in activities and programs

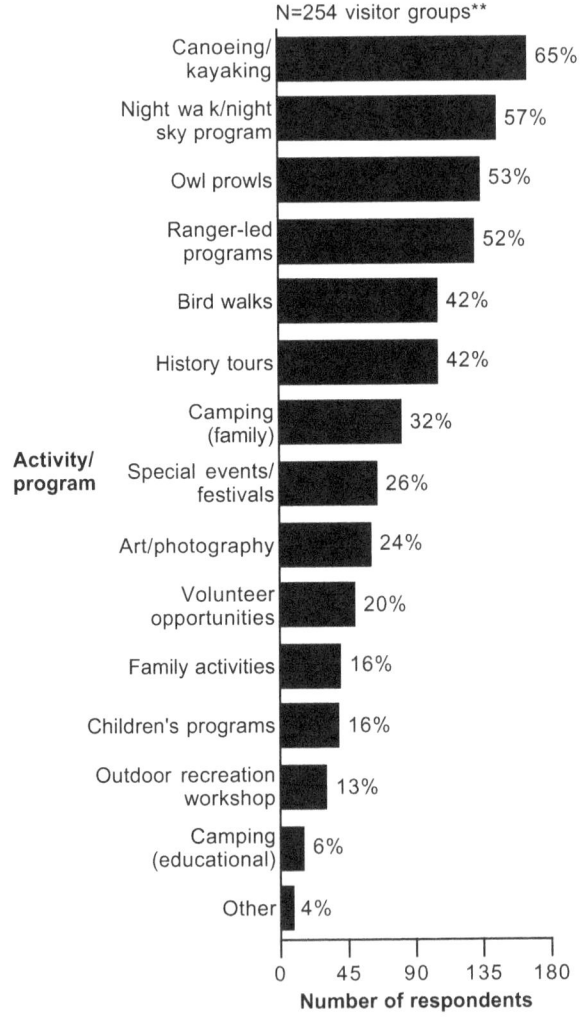

Activity/ program

Figure 86. Preferred activities and programs

*total percentages do not equal 100 due to rounding
**total percentages do not equal 100 because visitors could select more than one answer

Preferred topics to learn on future visits

Question 31

If you were to visit Congaree NP in the future, which subjects would you and your personal group like to learn about?

Results

- 95% of visitor groups were interested in learning about the park on future visits (see Figure 87).

- As shown in Figure 88, of those visitor groups that were interested in learning about the park, the most common subjects were:

  71% Plants/animals
  63% Champion trees
  58% Old growth floodplain forest
  56% History

- "Other" subject (<1%) was:

  Wildflower and tree identification

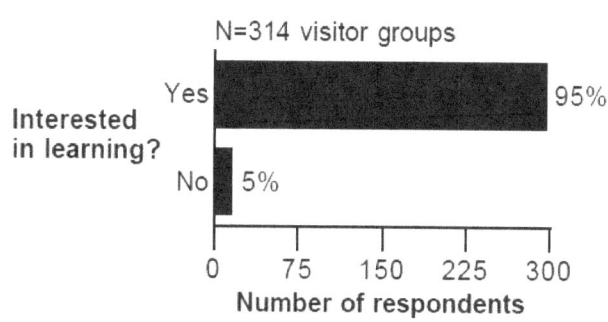

Figure 87. Visitor groups that were interested in learning about the park

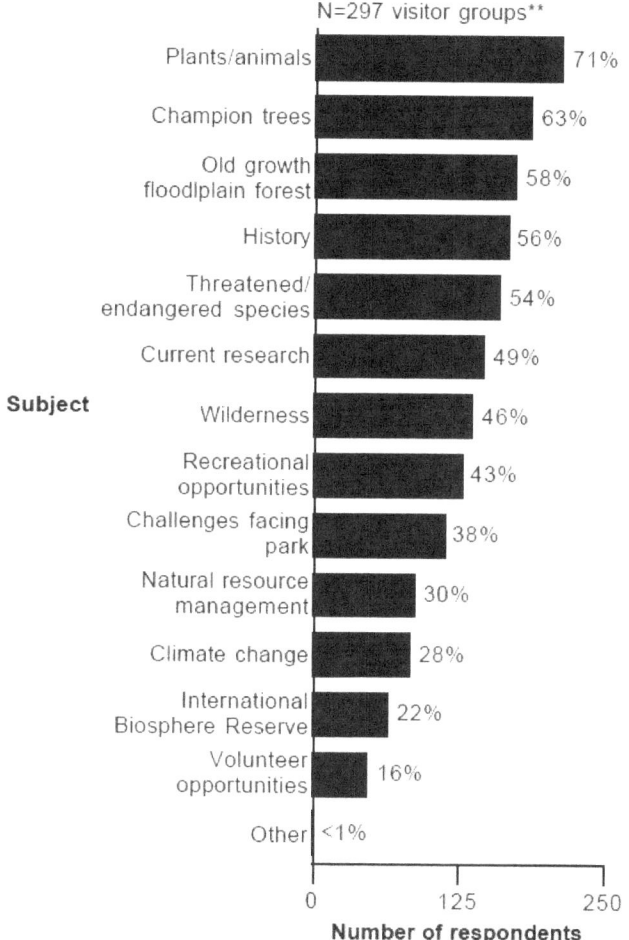

Figure 88. Subjects to learn on future visit

---

*total percentages do not equal 100 due to rounding

**total percentages do not equal 100 because visitors could select more than one answer

Overall Quality

Quality of facilities, services, and recreational opportunities

Question 27
Overall, how would you rate the quality of facilities, services, and recreational opportunities provided to you and your personal group at Congaree NP during this visit?

Results
- 98% of visitor groups rated the overall quality of facilities, services, and recreational opportunities as "very good" or "good" (see Figure 89).

- 1% rated the quality as "poor."

- No visitor groups rated the quality as "very poor."

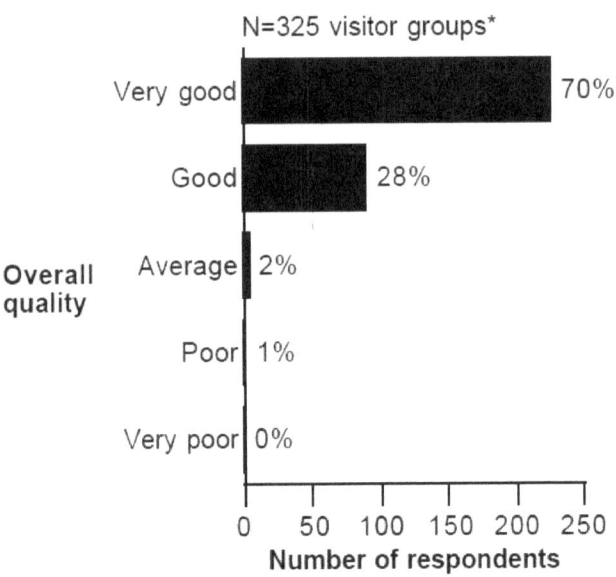

Figure 89. Overall quality rating of facilities, services, and recreational opportunities

Visitor Comment Summaries

What visitors liked most

Question 32a
What did you and your personal group like most about your visit to Congaree NP? (Open-ended)

Results
- 93% of visitor groups (N=306) responded to this question.

- Table 20 shows a summary of visitor comments. The transcribed open-ended comments can be found in the Visitor Comments section.

Table 20. What visitors liked most
(N=477 comments; some visitor groups made more than one comment)

Comment	Number of times mentioned
PERSONNEL (5%)	
Park staff	12
Rangers were helpful	5
Rangers were knowledgeable	2
Rangers were nice	2
Other comments	4
INTERPRETIVE SERVICES (6%)	
Boardwalk brochure	4
Ranger-led canoe trip	4
Self-guided tour	3
Learning about trees and their history	2
Naturalist talk	2
Walk Through History event	2
Other comments	14
FACILITIES/MAINTENANCE (23%)	
Boardwalk	48
Trails	31
Cleanliness	8
Visitor center	7
Trails well maintained	3
Other comments	11
POLICY/MANAGEMENT (3%)	
Uncrowded	5
Ability to bring dogs on trail	3
Other comments	5

Table 20. What visitors liked most (continued)

Comment	Number of times mentioned
RESOURCE MANAGEMENT (22%)	
Trees	17
Big trees	15
Cypress trees	9
Old growth forest	8
Unique ecosystem	5
Wilderness	5
Wild pigs	4
Wildlife	4
Birds	3
Old trees	3
Champions	2
Herd of deer	2
Knees	2
Loblolly pine	2
Plant life	2
Untouched forest	2
Weston Lake	2
Other comments	18
GENERAL (41%)	
Quiet	34
Solitude	23
Peaceful	14
Natural beauty	13
Walk	12
Hiking	11
Beauty	10
Beauty of fall foliage	7
Canoe trip	6
Cedar Creek	5
Everything	4
Fresh air	3
Nature	3
Pristine conditions	3
Camping	2
Interesting	2
Kayaking	2
Other comments	41

What visitors liked least

Question 32b
What did you and your personal group like least about your visit to Congaree NP? (Open-ended)

Results
- 63% of visitor groups (N=208) responded to this question.

- Table 21 shows a summary of visitor comments. The transcribed open-ended comments can be found in the Visitor Comments section.

Table 21. What visitors liked least
(N=231 comments; some visitor groups made more than one comment)

Comment	Number of times mentioned
PERSONNEL (0%)	
INTERPRETIVE SERVICES (5%)	
No canoe tour available	2
Other comments	9
FACILITIES/MAINTENANCE (23%)	
Clarify trail markings	5
Improve trail markers	4
Litter	3
Bathroom facility	2
Boardwalk needs maintenance	2
Lack of campsite with showers and restrooms	2
Parking lot full	2
Restrooms dispersed throughout park	2
Other comments	30
POLICY/MANAGEMENT (26%)	
Loud visitors on trails	15
Airplane noise	9
Crowded	3
Better road signs leading to park	2
Crowded canoe trips	2
Other comments	30
RESOURCE MANAGEMENT (9%)	
Did not see much wildlife	4
Wild pig ecosystem disturbances	4
Dry streams	3
Few birds seen	2
Other comments	7

Table 21. What visitors liked least (continued)

Comment	Number of times mentioned
GENERAL (38%)	
Nothing to dislike	39
Not enough time in park	10
Enjoyed visit	5
Rain	5
Enjoyed park	2
Loved it	2
Surrounding area	2
That we had to leave	2
Other comments	20

Significance of the park

Question 33
Congaree NP was established because of its significance to the nation. In your opinion, what is the national significance of this park? (Open-ended)

Results
- 83% of visitor groups (N=273) responded to this question.

- Table 22 shows a summary of visitor comments. The transcribed comments can be found in the Visitor Comments section.

Table 22. Significance of the park
(N=324 comments; some visitor groups made more than one comment)

Comment	Number of times mentioned
Old growth forest	44
Preservation	20
Trees	18
Preservation of forest	16
Preservation of ecosystem	13
Preservation of old growth forest	13
Old growth	12
Preservation of swamp	11
History	10
Unique habitat	10
Champion trees	8
Preservation of trees	8
Beautiful	7
Experience what nation was like once	7
Great significance	7
Preservation of local flora and fauna	6
Educating people about forests	5
Pristine wilderness	4
Important to have a natural area to visit outside the city	3
Last remaining river bottom land	3
Protected wilderness	3
The swamp	3
Unique biodiversity	3
Wildlife	3
Bald cypress	2
Cultural resources	2
Floodplain ecosystem	2
Great park	2
History going back to Native Americans	2
Maintain park for future generations	2
Old growth canopy forest	2
Opportunity for young people to learn	2
Size of the trees	2
Solitude	2
Tallest trees in the nation	2
Wilderness	2
Other comments	63

Planning for the future

Question 34

If you were a manager planning for the future of Congaree NP, what would you and your personal group propose? (Open-ended)

Results

- 69% of visitor groups (N=228) responded to this question.

- Table 23 shows a summary of visitor comments. The transcribed comments can be found in the Visitor Comments section.

Table 23. Planning for the future
(N=279 comments; some visitor groups made more than one comment)

Comment	Number of times mentioned
PERSONNEL (2%)	
More staff	3
Other comments	2
INTERPRETIVE SERVICES (21%)	
More canoe tours	8
More outreach programs	3
More tours	3
More information about champion trees	2
More information stations on boardwalk	2
More interpretive programs	2
More Native American history/perspective	2
Provide in depth guide to plants and animals	2
Other comments	34
FACILITIES/MAINTENANCE (25%)	
Expand boardwalk system	7
More trails	7
Campground with facilities	4
Campground	3
Repair boardwalk	3
Expand camping	2
Improve canoe launch	2
Keep maintaining boardwalk	2
More backpacking trails	2
Provide RV parking/camping area	2
Other comments	36

Table 23. Planning for the future (continued)

Comment	Number of times mentioned
POLICY/MANAGEMENT (29%)	
Improve/increase advertising	17
Expand park	15
Don't change anything	10
Continue protecting area	5
Continue allowing visitation	2
Do not commercialize	2
More recreational opportunities	2
Provide more canoe rentals	2
Other comments	25
RESOURCE MANAGEMENT (12%)	
Preserve the natural ecosystem	7
Eliminate/manage wild pigs	6
Control invasive species	3
Improve directional signage leading to park	2
Protect natural conditions	2
Reduce visitor impact	2
Other comments	12
GENERAL (11%)	
Nothing	7
Don't know	5
Keep up the good work	4
Other comments	16

Additional comments

Question 35
Is there anything else you and your personal group would like to tell us about your visit to Congaree NP? (Open-ended)

Results
- 54% of visitor groups (N=179) responded to this question.

- Table 24 shows a summary of visitor comments. The transcribed comments can be found in the Visitor Comments section.

Table 24. Additional comments
(N=279 comments; some visitor groups made more than one comment.)

Comment	Number of times mentioned
PERSONNEL (20%)	
Staff and volunteers were friendly	18
Staff and volunteers were helpful	17
Great staff and volunteers	8
Staff and volunteers were knowledgeable	6
Staff and volunteers were welcoming	4
Other comments	4
INTERPRETIVE SERVICES (8%)	
Enjoyed owl prowl	2
Other comments	21
FACILITIES/MAINTENANCE (4%)	
Boardwalk was very nice	3
Other comments	7
POLICY/MANAGEMENT (7%)	
More directional signage leading to park	2
Other comments	18
RESOURCE MANAGEMENT (5%)	
Trees	3
Other comments	11
GENERAL (56%)	
Thank you	26
Enjoyed visit	18
Great visit	16
Great park	12
Plan to return	8
Loved it	7
Keep it up	6
Beautiful	5
Fun	4
Love the park	4
Favorite place to visit	3
Wonderful	3
Good job	2

Table 24. Additional comments (continued)

Comment	Number of times mentioned
GENERAL (continued)	
Peaceful	2
Quiet	2
Other comments	37

Visitor Comments

This section contains visitor responses to open-ended questions.

Q32a. What did you and your personal group like most about your visit to Congaree NP?

- Ability to go into the wilderness
- Able to bring our dogs hiking with us
- Absolute feeling that one is traversing through Jurassic environs
- Abundance of cypress, boardwalk
- Always clean, great place to bring company/visitors
- Amount of land preserved as well as how well the boardwalk is maintained
- Assistance from park staff
- Awareness of variety of plant and animal life
- Bald cypress trees, Wise Lake, friendly people at visitor center
- Beautiful dog walk trails and boardwalks
- Beautiful facilities blending into the environment; wonderful boardwalk trail
- Beautiful fall foliage as well as fallen leaves
- Beautiful landscape and super friendly staff and rangers
- Beautiful scenery
- Beautiful trails
- Beautiful trees - I've never seen a landscape like this
- Beautiful, quiet, interesting
- Beauty
- Beauty
- Beauty and piece of the park as experienced on the elevated boardwalk
- Beauty and quiet
- Beauty and solitude
- Beauty and tranquility
- Beauty of fall foliage, streams
- Beauty of the Cedar Creek Canoe Trail; the peaceful solitude of it
- Beauty of the forest
- Beauty of the park
- Being able to be in nature on the boardwalk and having an easy travel
- Being able to see an old growth forest as no other prominent ones seem to exist in the eastern US
- Being away from the city
- Being outdoors on a beautiful fall day. Nice fresh air and peaceful scenery.
- Being outdoors, quiet, nice facilities, clean
- Being together in a beautiful place
- Being together is a beautiful natural environment that is not crowded with people
- Big trees
- Big trees
- Big trees and flood plain forest ecosystem
- Boardwalk
- Boardwalk

- Boardwalk
- Boardwalk
- Boardwalk
- Boardwalk - peace
- Boardwalk - you can walk and see the nature without paying attention to your steps
- Boardwalk and available wheelchair made the area accessible to physically challenged
- Boardwalk and hiking trails
- Boardwalk and the information in the boardwalk brochure. Very interesting. Loved how quiet it was.
- Boardwalk and tranquility
- Boardwalk gave freedom to explore without the worry of getting lost
- Boardwalk to the lake. Our 4 year old loved seeing all the spiders and walking sticks.
- Boardwalk trail
- Boardwalk trail
- Boardwalk trail
- Boardwalk trail and visitor center
- Boardwalk trail was top notch
- Boardwalk trail with literature provided
- Boardwalk trail, bald cypress
- Boardwalk trails
- Boardwalk, big trees
- Boardwalk, cypress trees and knees
- Boardwalk, guide to numbers on boardwalk
- Boardwalk, kayaking - peacefulness of park - very quiet season (11/1/11)
- Boardwalk, park personnel
- Boardwalks
- Boardwalks
- Boardwalks
- Bottomland forest
- Brochure with markers along boardwalks, easy walk
- Canoe trip
- Canoe trip and hiking trails
- Canoe trip on Cedar Creek
- Cedar Creek
- Chance to see very large trees
- Clean air, quiet, photo opportunities, beauty and mystery of Congaree National Park
- Clean park and very helpful staff
- Clean, quiet, peaceful
- Clean, thanks
- Convenient, quiet, beautiful place to stop for a break while on a bicycle tour
- Cypress nobs/knees
- Cypress trees
- Diversity
- Diversity of the trees from what we have at home
- Easy access to a large floodplain old growth forest

- Everything
- Everything the park had to offer
- Exercise
- Exploring nature
- Extensive trails, solitude
- Extent of boardwalk itself and the grand tour from it
- Fall colors
- Finding out about the trees and their history. Enjoyed the boardwalk, too.
- Forest
- Forest views
- Free canoeing, camping and hiking opportunities
- Friendly and helpful staff
- Full moon, cypress, campground layout, mosquito meter, large enough for number of visitors
- Getting out and walking in the woods
- Great hiking, saw wild pigs
- Great place for my Scout Troop; multiple opportunities for the boys to learn and use skills
- Great place to be
- Green time
- Hike on boardwalk trail
- Hiking
- Hiking
- Hiking
- Hiking and spending time with family. We came to see the wild pigs and got to see a few. We had a great time.
- Hiking on boardwalk, visitor center
- Hiking trails, boardwalks, lack of crowds
- History and environmental challenges of the park
- How remote the backcountry trails are
- I did not see anyone in the backcountry, exactly what I was looking for
- I liked that you were more dog-friendly than most NPs at least there were trails to walk them on
- I loved the boardwalk - especially that it was stroller accessible; that made it possible for even the little ones to visit
- Immense peacefulness and affect of frequent flooding on the landscape
- Immensity of the forest
- Information and natural state
- It was away from it all
- It was educational, serene and so relaxing
- It's a national treasure
- It's wonderful to have the resource so close to home
- Just a fun place. Lots to do, things to see, trails to hike.
- Just being in the outdoors together as a family
- Just seeing the trees (boardwalk, Wise Lake), quiet
- Kayaking Cedar Creek
- Kayaking Cedar Creek
- Knees

- Large bald cypress and other big trees
- Large old growth trees and forest
- Large trees
- Large trees
- Large trees, the quiet, the nature
- Learning about the cypress trees and their "knees"
- Learning about the uniqueness of the park
- Loblolly tree and cypress knees, boardwalks
- Loved everything
- Lovely walk in peace and quiet
- Low key atmosphere, clean trails and boardwalks, helpful rangers
- Mosquito marker
- Natural beauty and quiet. The remarkable trees.
- Natural beauty of the area
- Natural setting
- Nature led programs
- Nature walks
- Nice hiking trails, well sign-posted trails
- Nice trails; helpful staff
- Nice walk
- Nice walk and looking at forest
- Not crowded
- Old growth floodplain forest
- Old growth forest
- Old growth forest, plant and wildlife diversity
- Old growth trees
- Old trees
- Organization and the beauty of environment
- Our 2 year old granddaughter enjoying the big trees, birds (owls), squirrels, and big hollow trees
- Overall peace and quiet, fresh air, walking beneath the canopy of tall trees
- Paddle on Cedar Creek from Bannister Bridge
- Paddling Cedar Creek
- Pamphlet walking tour
- Park personnel, boardwalk interpretation, shared area history
- Park ranger at visitor center was very nice and helpful
- Park was designed to get you into the wilderness; the camping was walk in; it is free
- Peace and quiet, sounds of birds, owls, wild hogs
- Peaceful and quiet
- Peaceful family time
- Peaceful, beautiful
- Peaceful, clean, quiet. Park rangers were extremely nice and informative.
- Peacefulness
- Peacefulness
- Peacefulness along with the birds and insects chirping

- Peacefulness, campgrounds (hiked through all the vacant camps). Boardwalk trails were great. Indoor exhibits, too.
- Personnel
- Plenty of trails. Not crowded. Clean facilities. Accurate signage.
- Preservation
- Pristine conditions
- Quiet
- Quiet and being the only ones on the trail. It was natural, not accessible to non-exercisers.
- Quiet and solitude, except for leaf blowers for about 5 minutes
- Quiet area, huge trees, variety of trails, 2-mile boardwalk with interpretative booklet
- Quiet beauty
- Quiet visit with interesting environment that is unique to other national parks
- Quiet walk, peaceful setting, huge trees
- Quiet walk. "Knee" roots, which we've never seen or heard of.
- Quiet while walking the boardwalk
- Quiet wooded autumn atmosphere
- Quiet, its natural state
- Quiet, old growth forest, champion trees, birds, boardwalk, lack of trash, friendly staff
- Quiet, the wilderness, types of trees
- Ranger professionalism, maintenance of the boardwalk
- Ranger volunteer knowledge
- Ranger-guided kayak/canoe tour
- Ranger-led canoe trip
- Ranger-led canoe trip
- Ranger's help and the boardwalk and the quiet
- Record-breaking trees
- Safe, friendly environment to enjoy the outdoors
- Saw a herd of deer
- Seclusion
- Seeing the tall trees
- Seeing the trees and taking a walk on boardwalk. Ranger's talk.
- Self-guided tours were easy to follow. Very pleasant walking experience.
- Setting
- Showing daughter/granddaughter the outdoors via the wonderful boardwalks
- Sights were wonderful and the tour guide and administrative personnel were excellent
- Sights, sounds of the forest, the smell and the quiet
- Silence
- Size and age of trees
- Solitude
- Solitude
- Solitude
- Solitude
- Solitude
- Solitude and champion trees

- o Solitude and habitat
- o Solitude and quietness with an occasional sighting of deer and pigs
- o Solitude and the chance to see wildlife
- o Solitude and those old growth trees
- o Solitude during hike
- o Solitude off the boardwalk; I saw no other hikers
- o Solitude, beauty of changing leaves
- o Solitude, change of season
- o Solitude, pristine environment, staff
- o Solitude, serenity, beauty
- o Special event - walk through history
- o Spending time with my kids enjoying the beauty of nature
- o Staff
- o Staff and volunteers
- o Supplied equipment/canoes, etc.
- o Tall trees
- o Tall trees, extremely helpful Ranger O'Greely, unique look at climax forest
- o The whole experience was rewarding. Seeing the woods that had little human wear.
- o This park has a very nice visitor center
- o Three + days of no driving and lots of beautiful nature
- o Trail walk, seeing nature
- o Trails
- o Trails
- o Trails
- o Trails - elevated boardwalk, low boardwalk, the exhibits in the visitor center
- o Trails - marked well/maintained well; visitor center - staff friendly/great exhibits and shops
- o Trails and solitude
- o Trails and trees and water
- o Trails through the woods
- o Trails were great. It's nice having trails of different lengths.
- o Trails, coyote noises, close bathrooms, bluffs campsite
- o Trails, nearby
- o Trails, wildlife, quiet. There seem to be fewer pigs.
- o Tranquility
- o Trees
- o Trees
- o Trees
- o Trees
- o Trees and trails
- o Trees knees, walking tour of boardwalk
- o Trees were amazing; good trails and the quiet frequent sitting places along boardwalk
- o Trees, hiking, canoe trip
- o Trees, just seeing such large beautiful trees
- o Trees, the creek trip - astounding

- Unfamiliar ecosystem and hiking
- Unique beauty
- Unique environment
- Unique habitats
- Unique scenery, variety of trails
- Unique, uncrowded, recreational diversity
- Uniqueness of the NP
- Uniqueness of the park
- Unusual wilderness
- Varied scenes of nature visible from boardwalks - primitive campground
- Variety of plant life and unique ecosystem
- Variety of trails and walkways
- Variety of trails available
- Variety of trees and birds, fall colors of leaves
- Very accessible - my husband uses a cane or wheelchair
- Very clean, helpful, knowledgeable staff
- Very few people (visitors), the staff was extremely helpful and friendly
- Very helpful staff in the visitor center
- Very peaceful - seeing and learning about the trees
- Very peaceful and interesting
- Very peaceful except for the airplane and gunshot noise. We appreciate the way you have kept things so natural and almost primitive.
- Viewing bald cypress trees
- Visit lead by know naturalist (Rudee Manke)
- Visitor center & Karen on staff at desk was very helpful
- Visitor center was outstanding
- Visitor center, giant trees, Weston Lake overlook
- Visitor center, large loblolly pine, Weston Lake
- Walk on the boardwalk and trails
- Walking
- Walking along elevated boardwalk, following numbered items in brochure
- Walking boardwalk
- Walking the trails
- Walking the trails
- Walking the trails
- Walking through forest, seeing virgin climax forest
- Walking trails
- Watched a rat snake stalk a mouse and eat it. Saw a big hornets nest. Touched ancient loblolly pine trees.
- Watching the wildlife at the lake and looking at cypress knees
- We came to see the bald cypress trees, but enjoyed champions, park staff, canoeing/kayaking
- We love the "by the numbers" self-guided tours
- We loved everything. The ability to see all that exists there and still feel like we are by ourselves in the wilderness.
- Weather was great, quiet was nice

- Weather, boardwalk
- Well laid trails, absolute quiet, natural beauty
- Well maintained and marked trails
- Well maintained trails
- Well maintained trails and boardwalk
- Wilderness
- Woodpeckers - birds

Q32b. What did you and your personal group like least about your visit to Congaree NP?

○ A couple of loud walkers on boardwalk. There were two men - not adolescents or children.
○ Airplane noise
○ Airplane noise
○ Airplane noise
○ Airplane noises while hiking
○ Airplanes were a bit distracting and we didn't realize this is out of your control
○ Amount of wild pigs
○ Anole
○ Bathroom facility at campground
○ Being a swamp, we expected to see more water. It is not really a swamp. It is forest that floods for a few weeks a year.
○ Better advertised
○ Bluff Trail was marked with blue paint but merged with another trail also with blue and I got lost. The map on the bulletin board at the parking/camping lot did not help.
○ Boardwalk can be crowded and may not accommodate wheelchairs
○ Boardwalk seemed a bit rickety in places
○ Boardwalks in poor repair in some areas, particularly near visitor center
○ Campground
○ Campground - lack of water at the site. Lack of sites.
○ Can't think of any negatives
○ Canoe/launch area
○ Caught no fish, gravel in campground parking lot was noisy for sleeping in RV
○ Cement fiber boardwalk planks hurt feet. Natural wood boardwalk planks had spring and give.
○ Cold and rain
○ Could not spend enough time there
○ Couldn't find a third of the trail numbers that matched brochure numbers to read
○ Crowded parking lot
○ Cypress and knees not as big as advertised
○ Definition of old growth
○ Didn't have enough time
○ Didn't see as much wildlife as we had hoped to see
○ Directions to the park
○ Dirty port-a-potty at the after-hours campground needs replaced
○ Dogs being walked where they were not supposed to be
○ Dogs not allowed on boardwalk, but thrilled they were allowed in a national park.
○ Dry season, think it would have been better if water levels had been higher
○ Dry streams
○ Excellent weekend - all great portajohn @ campsite
○ Fill along the walkway/path
○ Four hour drive each way from Atlanta
○ Full parking lot
○ Gifts, shirts, etc., too sparse
○ Great experience

- Group of school students
- Hog destruction
- I don't know of any advertisement in Cola (30 min from park)
- Impact of wild pigs
- It was great, forgot to buy postcards
- It was perfect
- It was too short
- It would have been nice if we could have gone on canoes - lack of canoe available
- Kayakers stopped at the sandbar on the river trail
- Kids screaming
- Lack of a campsite with showers and restroom facilities
- Lack of native animals
- Lack of non-walk-in campsites
- Lack of restrooms on trail
- Large groups
- Leaving the park behind
- Liked everything
- Liked it all - exceeded expectations
- Littering on the roads leading to the park
- Long way to restroom if on other side of park
- Loud visitors on boardwalk
- Loved everything
- More bike trails needed
- More to do and see
- Muck
- My mobility to walk the trails. My problem, not one of the trails.
- Narrowness of trail/boardwalk
- New experience for us, boardwalk
- Newer, changing programs in visitor center would be nice, but wouldn't change our decision to visit
- No bathrooms at camping area. Very poor canoe launch areas.
- No birds
- No campground, just a parking area with no designated campsites
- No canoe tour available
- No complaints
- No dislikes at all. It's a great place.
- No dogs allowed on boardwalks
- No guided tours and no canoeing possible in November, even very good weather
- No major complaints
- No negatives
- No negatives
- No one had a complaint
- No RV hook-ups
- No tour items on Sims Trail
- Noise from other visitors

- Noise from the leaf blower
- Noise from trains
- Noise, loud talking from others, a real lack of respect
- Noisy kid
- Noisy kids
- Noisy visitors
- Noisy visitors, dogs off leashes
- None
- None
- None
- None
- None - can imagine visitor noise could be distraction if high volume
- Not enough time
- Not enough trail markers. Park maps need to be redone - more clear and more specific.
- Not enough trails and close parking
- Not enough wildlife
- Not much direction (signs) to exit. Wasn't sure where to turn to return to Columbia.
- Not much variety in scenery; least amount of time needed of all 29 NP I have been to
- Not so many animals
- Not sure
- Not sure - we really liked the park
- Nothing
- Nothing
- Nothing
- Nothing
- Nothing
- Nothing
- Nothing
- Nothing
- Nothing
- Nothing
- Nothing
- Nothing
- Nothing - all was fine
- Nothing - we still are anxious to see it all
- Nothing comes to mind
- Nothing comes to mind, really
- Nothing much, except the leaf blowing on one of the trails
- Nothing stands out
- Nothing, but I always imagine we'll see animals and it's rare to do so - deer, pigs
- Number of fallen trees
- Number of people
- Numbers of trail map guide difficult to see on boardwalk
- On a very busy day, parking could be an issue

- On the higher boardwalk too many people, too noisy
- Only criticism is that the parking lot for oversized vehicles needs more room to turn around an RV towing a vehicle. Impossible as it currently is.
- Other people
- Others on trails making noise
- Our canoe trip was too crowded - boats bumping in turns and couldn't keep close enough to hear the ranger
- Overnight camping area needs a good bathroom
- People walking the trails must learn to converse in whispered tones in order to possibly observe wildlife
- People who drove into park and do sin at whatever they wanted to do, loud radios, etc.
- Pigs
- Pigs are tearing up the backcountry very badly - signs almost everywhere
- Plane noise
- Plane noise
- Porta-potties, campsite signs from road, lack of firewood
- Rain
- Rain
- Rained - can't control the weather
- Rained on us half way around
- Ranger programs only on weekends
- Really no complaints
- Restrooms had powerful urine smell
- River Trail is poorly designed the furthest out point was an established utility road
- Road "trail" bisecting boardwalk with National Park Service vehicle. It ruined my wilderness experience. Plus crowds with running children.
- RV had to be parked away from the site in the parking lot, but it was free so it's okay
- Safety of the side walls of elevated boardwalk for toddlers, but not a huge problem
- Screaming kids, and the man who kept calling to his lost dog
- Self-guided maps did not have color of trails indicated on them
- Signage on trail is poor or non-existent
- Smoking near visitor center. Visitor sound of back up vehicle (staff) near picnic area.
- So much of park is inaccessible to hikers; more information needed for day hikers in backcountry
- Some groups did not respect the need for quiet and we heard gun shots while in the woods. We even saw a deer stand off the park's road before the parking lot.
- Some litter and office closed first time for my memory
- Some of the numbers on the interpretative trail were hard to see; we missed some
- Some of trail signs confusing
- Some visitors control of personal trash - recent 1-6 hours
- Somebody had a dog; people were talking loudly; somebody had a stroller that was very noisy on the boardwalk
- Sounds of all planes/trains
- Spiders
- Strange schedule of park video, i.e. that it was not available on demand
- Surrounding agricultural land, logging, chemical and nuclear industries

- Surrounding area
- That a backcountry camper can't have a fire, even with proper permits and training. It gets cold out there.
- That I had to leave when I did. It was a beautiful day.
- That it was wintertime and there were no leaves on trees
- That we couldn't stay longer
- That we couldn't stay longer due to our schedule
- The "no dogs allowed" signs
- The runner that was stomping along the boardwalk
- There was nothing not to like
- There was nothing that I disliked about the trip
- Time crunch of day
- To find the way to the park
- To learn that this national park doesn't support game management
- Too many people on canoe trips
- Tour length long
- Trail marking
- Trail signs were not very clear
- Traveled 13 miles from I-77 and only one road sign to notify drivers on distance to park
- Trip goes too fast. Not enough time to just relax and enjoy.
- Unleashed dog
- Very frustrating to find park. Locals are unaware of the national park and signs were poorly placed on interstate.
- Very impressed with everything
- Very little bird activity
- Very noisy family on the trail with us
- Vocally loud visitors on trail
- Walking
- We did not see the donation drop box like we usually see at other parks
- We didn't have enough time to enjoy the park to its fullest
- We enjoyed everything
- We had to back track the River Trail to get to sandbar because of lack of blaze/over grade
- We liked everything about the park. The canoe trip was great and the rangers made it unforgettable.
- We liked it all
- We loved it all
- We saw no animals and very few birds
- We were not able to spend more time and do more hiking
- Wild hog ecosystem disturbances
- Wish we could have gotten closer to the river. It was far, but we have something to come back for now.
- Wonderful solitude was broken by frequent jet plane roar
- Would have appreciated better/more obvious trail markers. Hard to discern with other people in front of us.
- Would have liked more information in brochure about items along boardwalk

Q33. Congaree NP was established because of its significance to the nation. In your opinion, what is the national significance of this park?

- A link to nature (as it was), history, biosphere, etc.
- A place one does not find much anywhere
- All parks are significant in efforts to preserve at least some of our natural/unspoiled areas
- Amazing trees
- An environment for study and reflection
- An understanding that important natural resources are in my own backyard
- Anyone that wants to see ole growth forest can see it
- Beautiful area of USA
- Beautiful forest
- Being able to see an old growth forest as no other prominent ones seem to exist in the eastern US
- Better signage directing to the park from several directions. Continue programs which educate locals and visitors about the park's significance to disappearing ecosystems.
- Big trees in southeast
- Biological, hydrological, cultural, geological and historic resources are a national treasure
- Bottomland flood plain ecosystem
- Can't wait to see it - the flooding
- Champion trees
- Champion trees
- Champion trees
- Champion trees, old growth, major drainage basin, cultural significance
- Champion trees, solitude and the birds
- Champion trees, very historical re: Civil War
- Climax forest unlike any other in such a large single tract
- Close to city, but far enough to feel like solitude
- Conservation and preservation
- Conservation of old growth swamp area
- Defines America
- Diversity bluff to floodplain
- Don't know enough
- East coast/south huge trees. Low country special area.
- Ecosystem and wilderness
- Exceedingly important
- Exposure
- Extremely significant - forest saved from extinction
- Few remaining old growth forest national parks in the south
- Floodplain protection; preserving old trees
- Floodplains, the old growth trees, the area's history, and to preserve
- Forest lands, wildlife
- Forest's importance to our nation
- Gives children/families an opportunity to experience swamp life
- Great park and beautiful wilderness
- Habitat and land

- Has some of the oldest trees in the U.S.
- Have never been in a NP like this one
- Having a place where people can experience what this country was like hundreds of years ago in this area. Preserving it for future generations.
- Historic, reflection of nature's resistance to human influences
- Historical and the trees
- Historical order of our state
- History and natural beauty
- History of the land leading back to the Indians
- History to preservation
- Huge save the old growth forests
- Huge trees, preserve ecosystem
- Huge. Historically important in US history and natural environment. Also, powerful story of how interested and committed people saved it from destruction.
- I do wonder why this is a national park instead of a monument. And I believe that government should not own land.
- I live in the city. It's important to me to have "natural" area to visit.
- I think it is quite rare and significant - one of a kind
- Important to recognize and maintain nature in original form
- Impressive forest; preserve unique habitat
- It has the largest bit of old growth floodplain forest here in the US
- It is a hidden gem. Great significance.
- It is a natural reserve which I hope can be maintained
- It is a piece of pristine forest
- It is a true sample of how the area was prior to white settlement
- It is a very significant area. Its nearness to Columbia increases its significance.
- It is an historical and rare ecosystem and located near such a populated area - it gives all the residents of Columbia a chance to enjoy nature
- It is an old growth, floodplain forest with beautiful sights
- It is beautiful
- It is found nowhere else in the US
- It is one of the last floodplain forests. Also has one of the highest canopy forests.
- It is the largest group of old growth floodplain forest in the world
- It is the largest intact tract of old growth river bottomland forest remaining
- It is very unique to our area. The vegetation.
- It preserves a unique habitat and gives people of differing physical ability a chance to experience the park
- It preserves the old growth bottomland hardwood forest, in which itself preserves so much
- It preserves the unique area
- It shows how we can protect our land and preserve our resources
- It's a park to preserve old growth forest with champion trees
- It's a place of great natural beauty that should be preserved for America's citizens
- It's a rare old growth floodplain forest
- Its beautiful and unique
- Its large old growth forest

- Its natural preservation
- Its rarity and the fact it is protected
- Its true history - Francis Marion probably did not travel through it. Trees/watery world there. The results of any research that might be able to bless/help our nation.
- Its unique ecosystem
- Keeping the land safe
- Knees of the bald cypress
- Large deciduous trees
- Large trees and swamp land show what the land used to look like before human intervention
- Large trees, cypress, etc. that have been allowed to grow and the importance of large swamp areas
- Largest and last stand of ancient forest in my homeland
- Largest old growth floodplain forest of its kind
- Largest remaining tract of Old Growth Bottomland floodplain with the largest trees in the trust
- Largest track of old growth floodplain forest in the USA
- Last major available area of its kind in the southeast
- Last of old growth
- Last remaining area of ancient hardwood bottomlands east of the Mississippi River
- Last remaining old growth floodplain forest
- Last remaining river bottom land
- Last remaining southeast old growth forest
- Last stand of bottomland forest
- Lets younger visitor see how the area used to look
- Loblolly pines and bald cypress "knees"
- Maintain nature for all to see for years to come
- Maintaining environment - untouched by man
- Maintaining old growth and education of leaving an environmental legacy
- Maintaining old growth floodplain plants and animals so we and future generations can experience them
- Maintaining the unique biodiversity now and in the future
- Major tourism attraction for South Carolina - natural resource based
- National champion trees, maintaining a floodplain park for us to experience
- National treasure
- Native trees and plants
- Natural area preserved for all to experience and enjoy
- Natural beauty, preservation
- Natural heritage
- Natural swamp atmosphere pertinent to South Carolina lowlands
- Needed wilderness preservation
- None
- Not enough time spent to answer
- Not many sights like this remain for the public to visit
- Not so sure; a lot of the Old Growth trees were destroyed by hurricanes and tornadoes
- Not US resident, therefore difficult to say
- Old growth
- Old growth and trails

- Old growth bottomland forest is something to be preserved. Any land not developed is important.
- Old growth canopy forest
- Old growth existence and area
- Old growth floodplain
- Old growth floodplain
- Old growth floodplain forest plants and animals
- Old growth floodplain forest, convenient from nearby large city
- Old growth floodplain forest. Pristine wilderness.
- Old growth forest
- Old growth forest
- Old growth forest
- Old growth forest
- Old growth forest
- Old growth forest and river on east coast
- Old growth forest floodplain
- Old growth forest was terrific
- Old growth forest, big trees
- Old growth forest, unique ecology
- Old growth forest; wetlands area
- Old growth forest. Also, the swamp and floodplain protection are very important to me.
- Old growth forests need to be protected
- Old growth southern forest
- Old growth swamp bottomland forest
- Old growth timber, wildlife, natural settings
- Old growth trees
- Old growth trees
- Old growth trees
- Old growth trees
- Old growth trees
- Old growth trees
- Old growth, native animals
- One can imagine the forests that existed before Europeans came to the Americas
- One of a kind
- One of the few old growth forests
- One of the few remaining natural growth forests
- One of the largest and last old growth bottom and basin lands in this country
- Our national forests are dwindling. Our culture is being uprooted.
- Our young people have such a limited opportunity to see and experience nature as it once was; all NP are truly a national treasure
- Peaceful floodplain forest; wildlife sanctuary
- Place to go where it is essentially the same for last 150 years
- Plants and animals living in this habitat that make it unique
- Preservation
- Preservation

- Preservation
- Preservation of big trees and swamp
- Preservation of forest resources for future generations
- Preservation of its unique ecosystem and champion trees
- Preservation of local fauna and flora
- Preservation of natural resources
- Preservation of natural spaces
- Preservation of nature
- Preservation of nature
- Preservation of old growth bottomland forest, wildlife protection
- Preservation of old growth, floodplain forest
- Preservation of old trees in river's flood zone
- Preservation of our growth forest
- Preservation of our natural heritage
- Preservation of remnant landscape
- Preservation of the old growth floodplain forest
- Preservation of the old growth stand, something not seen where I live
- Preservation of this old growth bottomland forest and its unique ecosystem
- Preservation of trees and floodplain
- Preservation of trees and swamps
- Preserve a unique environment, quiet
- Preserve eastern mixed hardwood flood plain
- Preserve floodplain forests, educate public on floodplain forests
- Preserve natural beauty for future generations
- Preserve natural habitat
- Preserve nature untouched
- Preserve old growth forest
- Preserve the old forest - provide nature learning experiences in the S.C. area
- Preserve wetlands and forest environment
- Preserving forest
- Preserving the land
- Preserving the old growth swamp
- Preserving what's left of this natural resource
- Progressive history
- Protect the old growth bottomland forest
- Protected old growth forest
- Protected wilderness to experience
- Protecting old growth trees
- Protecting the big trees and swamp
- Protecting the old growth floodplain forest
- Protection of the forest
- Protection of the old growth forest
- Protection of the old growth forest
- Protects a beautiful swamp

- Really special are the "landmarks" or areas - cypress roots, sugar cane, dwarf palmettos, lake.
- Remaining old growth deciduous forest is very rare. Congaree National Park protects this forest type.
- Remnant old growth hardwood swamp forest - trees and associated flora and fauna
- Safe this area from destroying, preserve seldom animals and plants, educate the people
- Save old growth trees
- Saving important natural habitat
- Scenery is very different. Not sure what type of animals are native, but it is a sanctuary for birds.
- Significance is exceptionally high. This is and must always be our nation's greatest investment. I enjoy the fact that my tax dollars are spent on this.
- Size of the trees
- Size of this forest and the age of many of the trees
- Size, age and diversity of trees and protecting the bottomland hardwood forest
- Snapshot of past forest; unique ecosystem
- So significant it must be preserved
- South Carolina the way it used to look
- Swamp
- Swamp Fox and trees
- Swamp is unique
- Swamp land - unique forestry
- Tall canopy
- Tallest trees in nation
- Teaches about swamps and bogs
- That it's a flood plain forest. Many other ones have been destroyed by development.
- That national parks exist in South Carolina
- The fact that the NP has some of, if not the, tallest tree canopy in the country
- The growth and trees
- They never cut down these trees like the rest of the land. It is real.
- This is a section of our country that shows how we were. Importance of nature. Collection of data.
- This old growth forest! How wonderful to have trees that have lived so long
- To be able to see virgin forest
- To enjoy
- To see some nature that has not been affected
- To show the history of the places that we go and to see how the world changes
- Trees
- Trees
- Trees, old growth, wetlands to be preserved. Also, bird habitats.
- Trees; diversity/scale
- Unique biodiversity
- Unique ecosystem/environment that people can easily enjoy
- Unique habitat
- Unique habitat preserved
- Unique natural environment
- Unique old growth preservation
- Unique qualities of the old trees and animal life

- Uniqueness
- Uniqueness of its biodiversity
- Very great
- Very important to preserve forever
- Very important to protect our national resources
- Very large area for old growth floodplain forest. Good example of multi-ecosystem across landscape.
- Very significant
- Very significant
- Very significant
- Very unique and different than parks out west
- Virgin forest
- Virgin old growth forest
- Virgin timber
- We must preserve old growth forests and educate people
- Wild forest
- With an increase in human development in our country, it's important to maintain as much wilderness as we can
- Wonderful example of few remaining floodplain, old growth hardwood forest
- Wonderfully natural
- Worth keeping

Q34. If you were a manager planning for the future of Congaree NP, what would you and your personal group propose?

- A campground
- A campground area with restroom/shower facilities, a bike trail
- A few more activities like mentioned
- A few more information stations on the boardwalk - wildlife, trees, etc. Different seasonal festivities. Horseback riding, especially fall, winter, early spring, available on a trail or two - maybe only available a few months.
- A live exhibit of the wildlife that you may encounter on the trail
- A lodge would be great
- A long trail that goes through the whole park
- A self-guided audio tour wireless with descriptions of all plants at dedicated locations. GPS reference points posted at intervals. We did not need them, but some visitors seemed confused as to their location and were hoping their phone would help.
- Acquiring more land, stopping environmental pollution upstream from chemical and nuclear.
- Add a small botanical garden close to the visitor center
- Add more boardwalks - add signs to inform visitors of the types of trees and plants
- Adding trail marker colors on tree signs along the trails. For every visitor center signs along the trails indicate distance to visitor center.
- Additional signs posted to assist in locating the park
- Additional to the park on the south side of the river
- Advertise about the park in the Columbia area
- Advertise in publications like Backpacker magazine to get more visitors to come to park
- Advertise more
- Advertise to the awareness of people. I think people (like me) would be interested. Canoeing/kayaking would be a great and unique attraction for this national park. Academic and educational activities for/of nature is nice and gentle, but can be a little dry for "fun and recreational" folks.
- Allow campsite reservations
- An RV parking and camping area
- Anything to help keep the natural conditions and environmental significance of the forest intact
- Ask people what they would like to see - keep up the good work
- At least one additional backcountry campsite - maybe along the Oakridge Trail
- Because of the scope of the park and the variety of activities, ensure that park staff are trained in first aid
- Better advertising; more staff to conduct tours
- Better awareness in the community
- Better maps and guide sheets
- Better promotion, expand kayak and canoe trips
- Better publicity - had never heard of this park before. Enchanted camping facitlites.
- Better signage on trails and keep up the good work
- Better trail markers
- Better/easier canoe put-ins
- Booklet with photos of plants and animals of Congaree National Park - with description of significance and scientific, local names
- Buy more land. Remove invasive plants/animals. Research.

- Campground - RV
- Campground with facilities. Visitor center should be a green facility - pervious drives and walkways.
- Canoe/kayaks - free rental. Update primitive campground bathroom.
- Changing out the timber on the boardwalks with composite boards
- Consider a shuttle for canoe trail. Run two or three times per day and charge a fee.
- Continue acquiring land buffers if possible
- Continue educating the public on why/how to protect this forest
- Continue its preservation and maintaining the boardwalk
- Continue repair of boardwalks
- Continue to maintain and preserve
- Continue to maintain beauty and access to public
- Continue to protect area
- Continue to purchase land as it becomes available
- Continue what you are doing
- Continued funding for the National Park Service
- Develop campground option - lack of showers, water
- Discuss the feasibility of adding bathroom facilities on the outskirts of the boardwalk trail. Improve boardwalk/interpretive trail markers, because we missed some. Perhaps have a detailed map that also outlines where to find the markers on the boardwalk loop trail.
- Don't know
- Don't know, everything was fine the way it is
- Don't know; didn't spend enough time there to say
- Downloadable MP3 walking tour. History of the park prior to Congaree.
- Due to popularity, fix the canoe launch as number 1 and increase camping sites
- Elevated boardwalk at least 30 feet in the forest trees. This would offer a truly unique view of the forest and instantly attract visitors.
- Encourage more people to visit
- Excellent park and facilities, so the only issue was airplane noise. What about establishing quiet hours for hiking in cooperation with nearby airport?
- Expand
- Expand camping and add bathhouse with showers. Separate RV and tent camping.
- Expand it
- Expand the boardwalk areas, build a tower to view the canopy top
- Expand the park
- Expand the trail system into the eastern portions of the park
- Expand visitor education of Native American history within the general area
- Expand/add observation deck/picnic area at Weston Lake. Add picnic area at Wise Lake. Make Kingsnake Trail a loop.
- Expansion of the park
- Expansion of the park, expansion of wilderness
- Extend network of trails east to US 601, overnight backpacking trail along Congaree River
- Extend the boardwalks
- Extend the park area
- Find a way to keep politicians from doing any damage
- Fish or hog hunting

- Flyers on what to look for
- Free kayaks
- Fundraising to buy adjoining land and expand. Link educational programs more to the high schools and emphasize high school "apprenticeships" or "internships."
- Give more history on land uses by Native Americans
- Great start - add to
- Guided hikes to discuss vegetation and animals
- Guided kayak trips
- Have visitor center sell approved firewood. It was difficult finding good dry wood in a swamp.
- Hunting of wild pigs
- I have no idea
- I think you're doing a good job balancing access to the park while maintaining the "wilderness" of the area. Keep doing what you are doing.
- I would "plant" more animals
- I would add canoe rentals on site
- Improve bathroom facility at campground; add canoe/kayak launch. Buy additional canoes/kayaks offer additional canoe/kayak tours.
- Increase staff
- Increased marketing to attract more visitors. Increased interpretive rangers' presence on trails.
- Information plaques along boardwalk. More information in visitor centers.
- It is perfect now
- Keep and enhance its preservation. Allow no motors or bicycles.
- Keep as natural as possible
- Keep doing things as you are
- Keep it "as is"
- Keep it as it is
- Keep it as natural as possible
- Keep it like it is
- Keep it like it is and add as much as possible
- Keep it safe, quiet
- Keep it the same
- Keep the park in its natural state and preserve trees; allow people to visit with minimal disruption
- Keep the website up to date. The calendar of events was not current when we checked.
- Keep up the good work
- Keeping the boardwalk well maintained
- Kill *Microstegium vimerium*. Make existing trails follow wilderness guidelines.
- Kill the wild pigs
- Label trees with botanical and common names
- Larger campground, more opportunity for canoe trips, better signage
- Let more people know it is here
- Limiting groups of kids
- Little additional development. If backcountry becomes crowded, implement permit system.
- Look for ways to make money. Better gift shop, camp store, canoe rental.
- Lots of family activities, more public relations and marketing to community
- Maintain beauty

- Maintain historical and natural plant life information availability to public
- Maintain it as-is and prevent too much infrastructure. Remove pigs.
- Maintain the boardwalk in top condition since most people use it
- Maintenance into perpetuity
- Make it bigger
- Making people more aware that it exists
- Manage feral and non-native animals and create managed hunts - feral hogs
- Manage invasive species
- Manage wild hogs. Should have archery only for hogs.
- Maybe a campground for a small amount of RVs, travel trailers
- Maybe boardwalks or guided walks. More elevated boardwalk trails, slightly better trail markings - add distances. Are there guided canoe trips?
- Maybe instruction or small signs reminding visitors to be respectful and quiet for others
- Maybe more tours, more history of the forest to be taught, what Indians used to live here
- Maybe open Weston Lake all day or at a set time with a ranger on patrol
- More access by car and trails
- More access to water through guided canoe trips, or easier accessibility for canoe rentals
- More activities with guides
- More advertising to acquaint public of facility and activity
- More advertising; residents are not aware the park is here
- More backpacking trails for multi-day trips
- More boardwalk trails
- More boardwalk trails
- More boardwalk trails
- More camping areas. Possibly a road that goes to the river.
- More canoe and owl trips, increase staffing
- More canoe trips available; more ranger-guided tours
- More diverse trails identifying trees
- More educational opportunities for children
- More educational programs/studies
- More effort on the control of invasive plants and animals
- More exposure
- More in-depth guides (paper) with more information about species, etc.
- More information about champion trees and ranger-guided access
- More information on website about times of ranger-led activities
- More informational signs along boardwalk trail – i.e., real signs rather than numbers
- More interactive activities during walk on boardwalk
- More interesting sites
- More interpretive programs like campfire chronicles
- More land. More land. Greenway as far upstream on (?) and downstream of (?).
- More national publicity, although I would hate to encounter more visitors
- More outreach and public education. More land protection, especially from road and bridge construction.
- More publicity of park and its attractions
- More recreation opportunities

- More recreation; on-site boat rental
- More robust visitor center explaining the park
- More tours
- More trails
- More trails
- More trails
- More trails
- More trails and backcountry camping sites
- More volunteers to maintain open water trails
- Multiculturalism, environmental education, wine/dine/hike
- Need more experience with park
- New campground with roads or driving lanes to each, water source there
- Night walks
- No changes
- No dogs or other pets in parks. Limit numbers of visitors on trails to prevent wear and littering. Keep champion trees a secret.
- No suggestions that I can think of
- None
- None
- None
- Not sure, more ranger-led things?
- Not sure, sorry
- Nothing
- Offering more canoe trips
- Open a pig hunt to reduce the population
- Outhouse/bathroom on longest trails. Larger parking area for canoe/kayak access. Closer parking, so distance to carry boat is shorter.
- Partnering with local outdoor clubs
- Perhaps a picnic area or maybe a music at night concert
- Perhaps expansion of the ranger-led canoeing trips within the park
- Pick up trash daily along trail. I saw old trash in 2 places.
- Possibly information along boardwalk instead of on pieces of paper?
- Potentially opening up different areas of the park to exploration
- Preservation of natural state with addition of a non-invasive camping area with shower and toilet facilities
- Preserve as much wilderness as possible. Make available with as little compromise as possible.
- Preserve it largely just as it is
- Preserve natural habitat
- Preserve natural state, educate in enthusiastic manner. Do not add commercial ventures.
- Preserve the native plants and animals
- Programs for occasional visitors. Improve a lot on information about what is special and where to find it.
- Promote value as environmental success story through efforts of local people
- Protect area and maintain access
- Provide water and dump facilities for RV's

- Providing camping areas other than primitive
- Publicize this park a little more
- Put in a small campground with designated sites with picnic tables and toilet facilities (pit toilets minimum)
- Raising money to buy more land adjacent to the park
- Remove the hogs. High water backcountry campsites for the canoe trail.
- Retain rusticity. No more building construction. Constrain hogs.
- Saving more land
- Selling the park to a private firm and no longer using tax dollars to support it. We need to drastically cut spending.
- Spread the news about this park's natural wonders
- Stay the course - great
- Sustainability and maintenance of existing facilities. No cuts.
- The continued and critical efforts to keep our rivers, Congaree, Saluda, etc., that is the life's blood of our park, clean and naturally flowing
- The film could show more about the park scenery and wildlife
- The park manager should limit the affect of humans on the environment as much as possible
- The signage on the boardwalk was not always visible
- Theme park activities
- To expand it as much as possible
- To increase the size of the park and to let the Bluff Trail forest grow naturally
- To keep as much of the park as possible natural. Reduce human interference and invasive species.
- To keep the Congaree National Park a pristine wilderness
- Trail signs could be a little better marked as to distances
- Trail without dangerous roots
- Try to get people of South Carolina to understand better the park's significance to them on the environment
- Was not there long enough
- We came from the east and the signs were non-existent until we were right at the park, otherwise it was a delightful time. Thanks for all you do to make this available to us.
- We enjoyed our day and the 3-hour drive was worth it
- Work on pig eradication
- Would love a canoe/walking tour during flooding

Q35. Is there anything else you and your personal group would like to tell us about your visit to Congaree NP?

o A fabulous place
o A sign indicating that there is a 'no dogs allowed' portion of the trail up ahead, so no one has to back track
o Absolutely love the boardwalk, maybe more information on trails with markers
o Additional canoe trip availability would be nice
o After this visit, we are planning to take my son's boy scout troop here. I just wish you took reservations for groups.
o Again, I just think it's a shame that this is the only large, old growth forest in the eastern US, but the visit was wonderful
o All employees very helpful and friendly
o All the park employees as well as other visitors were very friendly
o Always enjoy visiting
o Always love it. Great memories of family outings.
o Appreciated ranger's offer to show film and we watched it
o Beautiful park
o Beautiful resource
o Because it is a wilderness area it should promote "Leave No Trace"
o Congratulations. I will send all my friends here or at least try. Thank you.
o Consider a $2 campground fee
o Definitely keep the guided canoe trip
o Each time I visit I stand in awe of the peace and beauty of this place and hope it remains that way forever
o Enjoyable visit
o Enjoyed it a lot and found the staff to be enthusiastic and knowledgeable
o Enjoyed it so much
o Enjoyed it. Especially like "Mosquito Meter."
o Enjoyed our visit, thank the staff
o Enjoyed our walk and picnic
o Enjoyed the experience
o Everyone was so friendly and helpful. Thanks for all you do. We look forward to visiting you park again.
o Exceptional staff - most friendly and knowledgeable
o Favorite place to hike in the country. Always interesting, quiet.
o Fun and enjoyable
o Good job
o Grateful
o Great
o Great day; thank you for this treasure
o Great family trip. Staff was very informative and friendly.
o Great interaction with Congaree rangers/staff
o Great park
o Great park staff
o Great signage; we loved Congaree

- Great spot; great visit; thanks!
- Great staff at visitors center
- Great staff/great place to visit - a gem
- Great visit. Great park.
- Great, friendly staff
- Happy our tax dollars are sent here
- Help visitors find the champion trees
- I could not access the November calendar on the website and found out that there had been a computer glitch. Sorry I blasted you on the website survey.
- I have enjoyed Owl Prowls in the past; I don't wish to attend other activities
- I love Congaree National Park
- I love to bring visitors over from Europe to show this special nature areas of the park
- I only experienced the boardwalk trails loop. My responses may have varied had I seen other park trails. Good survey questions, but too many. It takes real interest and patience to answer that much.
- I plan to visit again sometime in the near future
- I was very pleasantly surprised going on the boardwalk. It was great. Also spoke with several rangers and they all were very friendly and extremely helpful. Wonderful experience and we will come back.
- I would put physical barriers after 9 pm or 10 pm to keep strangers out. Plus, perhaps a ranger hut or gatehouse to protect campers from strangers coming in during the night. The volunteer was a strange-acting man. He wanted to come and check on me in my van at 1 or 2 am.
- I'm glad this area got protected from urban development
- Increase gift shop to include other items found in national parks. Keep supply of 2009 Congaree National Park stamp series. They were out of the stamp for 2009 (passport to your national park stamp series).
- It is a great park - keep it up
- It is beautiful
- It is nice to take my kids to the same place my daddy took me when I was a boy
- It was a nice trip and we thank everyone who has made it possible
- It was a pleasant and amazing site
- It was fun
- It was great
- It was great
- It was most enjoyable, surrounded by the swamp
- It was rather boring except for Ranger Kate who was fun and full of information
- It was wonderful to see such old and healthy trees and plants thriving - keep it up! Thank you.
- It would be nice to provide at least minimal restroom facilities on the trails
- It's a very special place and the ranger was very friendly and informative
- It's one of our favorite places
- It's the perfect place to visit Thanksgiving morning
- Kathleen was one of the best rangers I have ever met. Kathleen was an amazing ranger who went out of her way to make sure we were educated and entertained. Thank you to her.
- Keep up the good work
- Keep up the good work
- Keep up the great work

- Knowledge gained was used in my daughter's college wetland essay
- Lots of fun. Wish I was able to come in summer.
- Love it
- Love your logo
- Loved it
- Loved it, especially looking at the large trees. Unfortunately, their leaves were so high up I had trouble identifying them. Perhaps a small plaque at bottom would help.
- Loved the free camping
- Loved the tall trees, fall colors, peacefulness, birds, lake and helpfulness of ranger Kathleen
- Need more historical interpretation
- Nice road trip detour. Would have liked to take my dog on boardwalk.
- Nice walk, very quiet, relieved stress, friendly and helpful park ranger
- Not at this time
- One of my favorite places to go
- Our ranger, William, was amazing. The Junior Ranger books were really too hard for the 2nd-3rd graders; there should be an easier form for younger children.
- Outstanding rangers and volunteers
- Overall, a very enjoyable and worthwhile experience
- Park personnel are welcoming, friendly and professional
- Park ranger Kathleen was very helpful, pleasant and knowledgeable about the park
- Pleasant, peaceful couple hours; will return when in Columbia
- Probably already have a monthly calendar of events on website. Identify animal sounds, meet the native animals of the Congaree.
- Rangers are friendly and knowledgeable
- Road maps are not adequate - need more road/direction signs
- Shorter survey
- Some of friendliest rangers we have encountered; Congaree is an untold story to so many
- Staff's presence at the visitor center is great, but I appreciate the solitude on the trail
- Super sweet park
- Thank you
- Thank you
- Thank you
- Thank you
- Thank you for a great visit
- Thank you for allowing me to celebrate my birthday in old growth bottomland forest
- Thank you for being there and keeping the park going
- Thank you for having us
- Thank you for letting us better experience the beauty of this earth
- Thank you for preserving such a special place
- Thank you for preserving such beauty
- Thank you for the Herculean efforts of those dedicated people, who realized a dream
- Thank you for the survey. We love this park and value this treasure. National Park Service should do this more often.
- Thank you for this park
- Thank you for your very helpful and devoted park rangers

- Thanks
- The beauty in South Carolina
- The boardwalk was very nice
- The law enforcement guy must stop sneaking up on people
- The national park was very clean and staff was very helpful
- The numbered "points of interest" along the boardwalks were quite interesting. The boardwalk is a soothing walk.
- The park ranger (wonderful woman from Duluth) and volunteer (guy formerly with weather service) were spectacularly helpful and welcoming. An absolute joy.
- The park rangers and volunteers were very kind and helpful. Basically, we were going to Bluffton to stay at our daughter's condo and knew that Congaree would be a possibility. Visited the Grand Tetons and Yellowstone in September.
- The paved parking area, the visitor center and the park service staff were excellent
- The people mentioned in answer to 29 should be commended. Super friendly, helpful and accommodating.
- The staff and grounds were great. Everything was clean and natural.
- The staff at visitor center were very friendly and helpful
- The staff was passionate and welcoming
- There was lots of life everywhere and the forest looked healthy
- This is a great park. Keep up the good work.
- This is a special forest deserving of preservation
- This is a wonderful site. Please upgrade campground for family use. It is not appropriate for many families - showers, water especially.
- This property is highly significant to the state and nation. So many children were around us with their parents learning about nature. There is so little old growth forest land left, we need to preserve more of it. Thank you.
- This was a wonderful and educational experience for us and hope we can visit again
- This was our first visit, but will not be our last
- Truly enjoyed
- Very enjoyable vacation; nice campground area; rangers were very nice, helpful, knowledgeable; really enjoyed ranger-guided kayak tour and hike (off trail) with park volunteer to champion trees - great prices/fees
- Very enjoyable, as always, except for loose dogs and shouting owners
- Very happy
- Very helpful and friendly park staff and volunteers
- Very neat park. Has wonderful natural resources. Enjoyed very much.
- Visit in November - temperature good, no bugs
- Visiting the park and Cedar Creek is like stepping back in time. Feel like I am the very first visitor.
- We appreciate that park access is free but still well-staffed and maintained
- We enjoyed it
- We enjoyed it very much and plan to come again with more family and friends
- We enjoyed it very much. Great exhibits at the visitor center, including the movie.
- We enjoyed learning about the park from talking to ranger "Corrine" in the visitor center
- We enjoyed our first day so much we decided to stay (camp) another night - wonderful
- We enjoyed the visit. Would have liked greater access to water activities.
- We had a blast. See you soon.

- We had a great time
- We had a great time. Good exercise signs and signs to the park were nonexistent.
- We had limited time to acquaint ourselves and walk elevated boardwalk. Next time, we will do one or more of the trails.
- We have loved visiting several times. I like that there is a national park in this region, not all out west.
- We love Congaree National Park and enjoy visiting
- We love this park
- We loved it
- We loved it
- We loved our visit. What a gem.
- We may suggest some emergency call boxes along the boardwalk in case of medical emergency
- We really had the best time. I can't thank you enough.
- We spent a pleasant couple of hours in the NP that we wouldn't have found elsewhere
- We think you're doing a great job and we love to visit multiple times a year
- We wanted to go canoeing, but it was unclear how to do so. It looked like we needed to book months in advance, but we did not plan our trip so far in advance.
- We were so surprised at how beautiful and unique the park is
- We were visiting Columbia and wanted to walk. Had two strollers. I suggested the park. It was very nice. Thank you.
- We will be back
- We wish we would have seen wild pigs
- We're happy the area was preserved so those who are unaware of its existence (us) can see it
- What Congaree lacks in majesty is made up by the personal service of rangers. Personnel-guided canoe trip was wonderful and cheap. Also made my son's day to become a Junior Ranger.
- Willing to archery hunt wild hogs on a volunteer basis; office closed Thanksgiving Day so most services were not available; first time in many years I remember it closed. For over 30 years friends and family have 'walked off' Thanksgiving lunch making room for dinner. Loved our Owl Prowl and Rudy Marke (unreadable) walk
- Wonderful
- Wonderful place. I bring my students here as a reward at the end of each semester.
- Wonderful. Thank you.
- Would enjoy hearing more about park area ties to human development in South Carolina
- Would like to know we could have gone off trail
- You are doing good, thank you and shalom
- Your staff was outstanding. They were excited to introduce us to the highlights of the park. We would recommend this experience to family and friends.

Appendix 1: The Questionnaire

United States Department of the Interior

NATIONAL PARK SERVICE
Congaree National Park
100 National Park Road
Hopkins, SC 29061

IN REPLY REFER TO:

Dear Visitor:

Thank you for participating in this important study. Our goal is to learn about the expectations, opinions, and interests of visitors to Congaree National Park. This information will assist us in our efforts to better manage this park and to serve you.

This questionnaire is only being given to a select number of visitors, so your participation is very important! It should only take about 20 minutes after your visit to complete.

When your visit is over, please complete this questionnaire. Seal it in the postage paid envelope provided and drop it in any U.S. mail box.

If you have any questions, please contact Margaret Littlejohn, NPS VSP Director, Park Studies Unit, College of Natural Resources. P.O. Box 441139, University of Idaho. Moscow, Idaho 83844-1139, phone: 208-885-7863, email : ttej@uidaho.edu.

We appreciate your help.

Sincerely,

Tracy Swartout
Superintendent

Social Science Program
National Park Service
U.S. Department of the Interior

Visitor Services Project

Congaree National Park

Visitor Study

4

Your Visit To Congaree National Park

NOTE: n th s quest onna re your **personal group** s def ned as anyone that you are v s t ng the park w th such as spouse fam y fr ends etc. Th s does not nc ude the arger group that you m ght be trave ng w th such as schoo church scouts or tour group.

1. Pr or to your v s t, how d d you and your persona group obta n nformat on about Congaree Nat ona Park (NP)? P ease mark (●) **all that app y.** ➔ **Go to question 2**

- ○ D d not obta n nformat on pr or to v s t
- ○ Chamber of commerce/v s tors bureau/state we come center
- ○ Congaree NP webs te: www.nps.gov/cong
- ○ Other webs tes — Wh ch one(s)? _____
- ○ Fr ends/re at ves/word of mouth
- ○ H ghway s gns
- ○ Inqu ry to park v a phone, ma   or e-ma
- ○ Loca bus nesses (hote s, mote s, restaurants, etc.)
- ○ Maps/brochures
- ○ Newspaper/magaz ne art c es
- ○ Other Nat ona Park Serv ce s tes
- ○ Prev ous v s ts
- ○ Schoo c ass/program
- ○ Soc a med a (such as Facebook, Tw tter, etc.)
- ○ Te ev s on/rad o programs/v deos
- ○ Trave gu des/tour books (such as AAA, etc.)
- ○ Other (P ease spec fy) _____

2. Pr or to your v s t, were you and your persona group aware of programs (ranger- ed wa ks, canoe tr ps, presentat ons, schoo group tours, etc.) offered n Congaree NP?

   ○ Yes   ○ No

3

DIRECTIONS

1) P ease have the se ected nd v dua (at east 16 years o d) comp ete th s quest onna re.

2) Answer the quest ons carefu y s nce each quest on s d fferent.

3) For quest ons that use c rc es (○), p ease mark your answer by f   ng n the c rc e w th b ack or b ue nk. P ease do not use penc .

   Like this: Not like this:

4) Sea t n the postage pa d enve ope prov ded.

5) Drop t n a U.S. ma box.

Thank you!

PRIVACY ACT and PAPERWORK REDUCTION ACT statement:

3. a) In 2003, Congaree Swamp National Monument became Congaree NP. Did this name change have any effect on your decision to visit?

   ○ Yes   ○ No   ○ Not sure

   b) If YES, what effect did it have? Please be specific. _____

4. a) Prior to your visit, were you aware of what congressionally designated wilderness is?

   ○ Yes   ○ No   ○ Not sure

   b) If NO, did you and your personal group learn about congressionally designated wilderness during your visit?

   ○ Yes   ○ No

5. The National Park Service has a policy to control or remove non-native plants and animals from within park boundaries. Non-native species occupy an area that is not part of their natural, historic range, and often originated from another continent or region. Many of these species are invasive and damage park resources. Were you aware of this policy prior to your visit to Congaree NP?

   ○ Yes   ○ No   ○ Not sure

6. Would you and your personal group be supportive of the control and removal of non-native species at Congaree NP? Please mark (●) only one for each option.

	Yes	No	Not sure
a) Non-native plants	○	○	○
b) Non-native animals	○	○	○

7. On this trip, what was the **primary** reason that you and your personal group came to the Congaree NP **area** (within 1-hour drive of the park)? Please mark (●) **only one.**

   ○ Resident of the area (within 1-hour drive of the park) → **Go to Question 8**

   ○ Visit Congaree NP

   ○ Visit other attractions in the area

   ○ Visit friends/relatives in the area

   ○ Traveling through – unplanned visit

   ○ Business

   ○ Other (Please specify) _____

8. On this visit, which sites did you and your personal group visit in the Congaree NP **area** (within 1-hour drive of the park)? Please mark (●) **all that apply.**

   ○ EdVenture   ○ Columbia Metropolitan Airport

   ○ Lake Murray   ○ Columbia Museum of Art

   ○ National Advocacy Center   ○ Ft. Jackson Army Training Center

   ○ Riverbanks Zoo   ○ Harbison State Forest

   ○ Shaw Air Force Base   ○ The State Capitol

   ○ South Carolina State Museum   ○ University of South Carolina

   ○ South Carolina State Parks

   ○ Other (Please specify) _____

9. a) On this trip, did you and your personal group stay overnight away from your **permanent residence** either inside Congaree NP or within the nearby area (within 1-hour drive of the park)?

   ○ Yes   ○ No → **Go to Question 10**

   b) and c) If YES, how many nights did you and your personal group spend in the following types of accommodations? Please write the number of nights stayed.

   b) Number of nights inside park   **c) Number of nights outside park within 1-hour drive**

   n/a _____ Lodge, hotel, motel, cabin, rented condo/home, or bed & breakfast _____

   _____ RV/trailer camping _____

   _____ Tent camping _____

   _____ Backcountry camping

   n/a _____ Personal seasonal residence _____

   n/a _____ Residence of friends or relatives _____

   _____ Other accommodations (Please specify below) _____

   _____

   Inside park _____   Outside park _____

10. a) On this visit to Congaree NP, did you and your personal group walk/canoe/kayak any park trails?

   ○ Yes   ○ No → **Go on to Question 11**

b) If YES, which of the following trails did you and your personal group walk/canoe/kayak on this visit? Please mark (●) all that apply.

- ○ Cedar Creek Wilderness Canoe Trail
- ○ Elevated Boardwalk Trail
- ○ Low Boardwalk Trail
- ○ Oakridge Trail
- ○ Weston Lake Loop Trail
- ○ Other (Please specify) _____
- ○ Bluff Trail
- ○ Kingsnake Trail
- ○ River Trail
- ○ Sims Trail

11. On this visit, in which activities did you and your personal group participate within Congaree NP? Please mark (●) all that apply.

- ○ Citizen Science program
- ○ Exercising (jogging, rollerblading, etc.)
- ○ Nature study (other than birdwatching)
- ○ Ranger-led programs
- ○ Visiting the visitor center
- ○ Walking dogs
- ○ Walking/hiking
- ○ Other (Please specify) _____
- ○ Backpacking
- ○ Birdwatching
- ○ Camping
- ○ Canoeing/kayaking
- ○ Fishing
- ○ Park special event
- ○ Picnicking

12. On this visit, how many vehicles did you and your personal group use to arrive at the park? Please write "0" if you did not arrive by vehicle.

_____ Number of vehicles

13. a) How long did you and your personal group stay in the Congaree NP area (within 1-hour drive of the park)? Please estimate partial hours/days as ¼, ½, ¾.

○ Resident of the area ➔ **Go to part b of this question on next page**

_____ Number of hours **if less than 24 hours**
- OR -
_____ Number of days **if 24 hours or more**

---

b) On this visit, how long did you and your personal group spend visiting Congaree NP? Please estimate partial hours/days as ¼, ½, ¾.

_____ Number of hours **if less than 24 hours**
- OR -
_____ Number of days **if 24 hours or more**

14. It is the National Park Service's responsibility to protect Congaree NP's natural, scenic, and cultural resources while at the same time providing for public enjoyment. How important is protection of the following resources/attributes in the park to you and your personal group? Please mark (●) one answer for each resource/attribute.

Resource/attribute	Not important	Somewhat important	Moderately important	Very important	Extremely important
Clean air (visibility)	○	○	○	○	○
Clean water	○	○	○	○	○
Clear night sky (star gazing)	○	○	○	○	○
Cultural history (photographs/artifacts/oral histories)	○	○	○	○	○
Designated wilderness/backcountry	○	○	○	○	○
Educational opportunities	○	○	○	○	○
Historic buildings/archeological sites	○	○	○	○	○
Native plants	○	○	○	○	○
Native wildlife	○	○	○	○	○
Natural quiet/sounds of nature	○	○	○	○	○
Parking availability	○	○	○	○	○
Recreational opportunities	○	○	○	○	○
Scenic views	○	○	○	○	○
Solitude	○	○	○	○	○

15. a) Prior to this visit were you and your personal group aware that Congaree NP is home to the Old-Growth Bottom and Forest Research and Education Center, one of 21 centers nationwide?

○ Yes   ○ No

b) Did you and your personal group notice any scientists, scientific markers, or scientific equipment at work while you were in the park?

○ Yes   ○ No

c) Did you and your personal group – through programs and products – learn about actual results of scientific studies at the park?

○ Yes   ○ No

16. a) Please mark (●) all of the information services and facilities that you or your personal group **used** at Congaree NP during this visit.

b) For only those services and facilities that you or your personal group **used,** please rate their importance to your visit from 1-5.

c) For only those services and facilities that you or your personal group **used,** please rate their quality from 1-5.

b) If used, how important?
1=Not important
2=Somewhat important
3=Moderately important
4=Very important
5=Extremely important

c) If used, what quality?
1=Very poor
2=Poor
3=Average
4=Good
5=Very good

a) Information services/facilities used? Mark (●)

○ Assistance from park staff

○ Assistance from park volunteers

○ Bulletin boards

○ Junior or Ranger program

○ Park brochure/map

○ Park interpretive pamphlets

○ Park newspaper *Boardwalk Talk*

○ Park website (nps.gov/cong) used before or during visit

○ Ranger-led talks/programs/walks

○ Ranger-guided canoe tours

○ Visitor center bookstore sales items (section, price, etc.)

○ Visitor center videos/films/movies

○ Visitor center exhibits

17. a) Please mark (●) **all** of the visitor services and facilities that you or your personal group **used** at Congaree NP during this visit.

b) For only those services and facilities that you or your personal group **used,** please rate their importance to your visit from 1-5.

c) For only those services and facilities that you or your personal group **used,** please rate their quality from 1-5.

b) If used, how important?
1=Not important
2=Somewhat important
3=Moderately important
4=Very important
5=Extremely important

c) If used, what quality?
1=Very poor
2=Poor
3=Average
4=Good
5=Very good

a) Visitor services/facilities used? Mark (●)

○ Access for people with disabilities

○ Backcountry camping

○ Boardwalks

○ Campgrounds

○ Canoe launches

○ Directional signs outside park

○ Park directional signs

○ Parking areas

○ Picnic areas

○ Restrooms

○ Trails

18. On this visit, were you and your personal group part of the following types of organized groups?

a) Commercial guided tour group   ○ Yes   ○ No

b) School/educational group   ○ Yes   ○ No

c) Other (scouts, work, church, etc.)   ○ Yes   ○ No

d) If you were with one of these organized groups, how many people, including yourself, were in this group?

_____ Number of people in organized group

19. a) On this visit, what kind of personal group (not guided tour/school/other organized group) were you with?

- ◯ Alone
- ◯ Family
- ◯ Other (Please specify) _____
- ◯ Friends
- ◯ Family and friends

b) On this visit, how many people were in your personal group, including yourself?

_____ Number of people

20. For you and your personal group on this visit, please provide the following. (If you do not know the answer, leave blank).

	a) Current age	b) U.S. ZIP code or name of country other than U.S.	Number of visits to Congaree NP (including this visit) c) Past 12 months	d) Lifetime	Number of visits to other National Parks (including this visit) e) Past 12 months	f) Lifetime
Yourself	___	___	___	___	___	___
Member #2	___	___	___	___	___	___
Member #3	___	___	___	___	___	___
Member #4	___	___	___	___	___	___
Member #5	___	___	___	___	___	___
Member #6	___	___	___	___	___	___
Member #7	___	___	___	___	___	___

21. For you only, what is the highest level of education you have completed? Please mark (•) one.

- ◯ Some high school
- ◯ High school diploma/GED
- ◯ Some college
- ◯ Bachelor's degree
- ◯ Graduate degree

22. a) Does anyone in your personal group have mobility or other physical impairments?

- ◯ Yes
- ◯ No ➜ **Go on to Question 23**

b) If YES, did anyone in your personal group have a physical condition that made it difficult to access or participate in park activities or services?

- ◯ Yes
- ◯ No

23. a) Are you or members of your personal group Hispanic or Latino? Please mark (•) **one** for each group member.

	Yourself	Member #2	Member #3	Member #4	Member #5	Member #6	Member #7
Yes Hispanic or Latino	◯	◯	◯	◯	◯	◯	◯
No not Hispanic or Latino	◯	◯	◯	◯	◯	◯	◯

b) What is your race? What is the race of each member of your personal group? Please mark (•) **one or more** for you and each group member.

	Yourself	Member #2	Member #3	Member #4	Member #5	Member #6	Member #7
American Indian or Alaska Native	◯	◯	◯	◯	◯	◯	◯
Asian	◯	◯	◯	◯	◯	◯	◯
Black or African American	◯	◯	◯	◯	◯	◯	◯
Native Hawaiian or other Pacific Islander	◯	◯	◯	◯	◯	◯	◯
White	◯	◯	◯	◯	◯	◯	◯

24. a) On this trip, if you and your personal group had not chosen to visit Congaree NP, what other recreation site would you have visited instead?

_____

b) How far is this alternative site from your home? _____ miles

25. a) Which category best represents your annual **household** income? Please mark (•) **only one.**

- ◯ Less than $24,999
- ◯ $25,000-$34,999
- ◯ $35,000-$49,999
- ◯ $100,000-$149,999
- ◯ $50,000-$74,999
- ◯ $75,000-$99,999
- ◯ $150,000-$199,999
- ◯ $200,000 or more
- ◯ Do not wish to answer

b) How many people are in your household? _____ Number of people

c) Did your household take any unpaid vacation or take unpaid time off of work to come on this trip?

- ◯ Yes
- ◯ No

29. P ease nd cate how the fo ow ng e ements may have affected you and your persona group's park exper ence dur ng th s v s t to Congaree NP. P ease mark (●) **only one for each e ement.**

Affect your park experience?	Detracted from	No effect	Added to	D d not experience
A rp ane no se	○	○	○	○
Automob e no se	○	○	○	○
Gunshots from ne ghbor ng ands	○	○	○	○
No se from park staff act v t es (such as chainsaws leaf blowers generators etc)	○	○	○	○
Tra n no se	○	○	○	○
Other v s tors' act v t es	○	○	○	○
Sma number of v s tors on tra s	○	○	○	○
Large number of v s tors on tra s	○	○	○	○
Sma number of v s tors canoe ng/kayak ng	○	○	○	○
Large number of v s tors canoe ng/kayak ng	○	○	○	○
Impact of w d p gs	○	○	○	○
Other (P ease spec fy)	○	○	○	○

30. If you were to v s t Congaree NP n the future, wh ch types of organ zed act v t es and programs wou d you and your persona group ke to have ava ab e? P ease mark (●) **all that app y.**

○ Not nterested n organ zed act v t es/programs → **Go on to Question 31**

○ Art/photography

○ B rd wa ks

○ N ght wa k/n ght sky program

○ Camp ng (fam y)

○ Outdoor recreat on workshop

○ Camp ng (educat ona)

○ Ow prow s

○ Canoe ng/kayak ng

○ Ranger- ed programs

○ Ch dren's programs

○ Spec a events/fest va s

○ Fam y act v t es

○ Vo unteer opportun t es (ways to he p the park)

○ Other (P ease spec fy) _____

---

26. For you and your persona group, p ease est mate a expend tures for the tems sted be ow for th s v s t to Congaree NP and the surround ng **area** (w th n 1-hour dr ve of the park). **Please write "0" if no money was spent in a particular category.**

a) P ease st your persona group's tota expend tures ns de Congaree NP.

b) P ease st your persona group's tota expend tures n the **surrounding area** outs de the park (w th n 1-hour dr ve of the park).

NOTE: Surround ng area res dents shou d on y nc ude expend tures that were **just for this trip** to Congaree NP.

EXPENDITURES

	a) Inside park	b) Outside park
Lodges, hote s, mote s, cab ns, B&B, etc.	n/a	$____
Camp ng fees and charges	n/a	$____
Canoe/kayak renta charges	n/a	$____
Gu de fees and charges	n/a	$____
Restaurants and bars	n/a	$____
Grocer es and takeout food	n/a	$____
Gas and o (auto, RV, boat, etc.)	n/a	$____
Other transportat on expenses (renta cars, tax s, auto repa rs, but NOT a rfare)	n/a	$____
Adm ss on, recreat on, enterta nment fees	n/a	$____
A other purchases (souven rs, f m, books, sport ng goods, c oth ng, etc.)	$____	$____
Donat ons	$____	$____

c) How many peop e do the above expenses cover?

____ Adu ts (18 years or over)   ____ Ch dren (under 18 years)

P ease wr te "0" f no ch dren were covered by the expend tures.

27. Overa , how wou d you rate the qua ty of the fac t es, serv ces, and recreat ona opportun t es prov ded to you and your persona group at Congaree NP dur ng th s v s t? P ease mark (●) **one.**

Very poor	Poor	Average	Good	Very good
○	○	○	○	○

28. Wou d you and your group be ke y to v s t Congaree NP aga n n the future?

○ Yes   ○ No   ○ Not sure

BUSINESS REPLY MAIL
FIRST CLASS MAIL   PERMIT NO. 163   MOSCOW ID

POSTAGE WILL BE PAID BY ADDRESSEE

VISITOR SERVICE PROJECT
PARK STUDIES UNIT
COLLEGE OF NATURAL RESOURCES
UNIVERSITY OF IDAHO
875 PERIMETER DRIVE
MOSCOW ID 83843-9960

GTK6708M

PO 1139

31. If you were to v s t Congaree NP n the future, wh ch subjects wou d you and your
persona group ke to earn about? P ease mark (●) **all that app y.**

O   Not nterested n earn ng about these subjects → **Go to Question 32**

O   Cha enges fac ng park

O   Champ on trees

O   C mate change

O   Current research

O   H story

O   Internat ona B osphere Reserve

O   Natura resource management

O   O d growth f oodp a n forest

O   P ants/an ma s

O   Threatened/endangered spec es

O   Vo unteer opportun t es
     (ways to he p the park)

O   W derness

O   Recreat ona opportun t es (canoe ng/kayak ng, f sh ng, camp ng, etc.)

O   Other (P ease spec fy) _____

32. a) What d d you and your persona group ke **most** about your v s t to Congaree NP?

_____

b) What d d you and your persona group ke **least** about your v s t to Congaree NP?

_____

33. Congaree NP was estab shed because of ts s gn f cance to the nat on. In your
op n on, what s the nat ona s gn f cance of th s park?

_____

34. If you were a manager p ann ng for the future of Congaree NP what wou d you and
your persona group propose?

_____

35. Is there anyth ng e se you and your persona group wou d ke to te us about your
v s t to Congaree NP?

_____

Thank you for your he p! P ease sea the quest onna re n the postage pa d enve ope
prov ded and drop t n any U.S. ma box.   ♻ Printed on recycled paper

Appendix 2: Additional Analysis

The Visitor Services Project (VSP) offers the opportunity to learn from VSP visitor study data through additional analysis. Two-way and three-way cross tabulations can be made with any questions.

Below are some examples of the types of cross tabulations that can be requested. To make a request, please use the contact information below, and include your name, address and phone number in the request.

1. What proportion of family groups with children attends interpretive programs?

2. Is there a correlation between visitors' ages and their preferred sources of information about the park?

3. Are highly satisfied visitors more likely to return for a future visit?

4. How many international visitors participate in hiking?

5. What ages of visitors would use the park website as a source of information on a future visit?

6. Is there a correlation between visitor groups' rating of the overall quality of their park experience and their ratings of individual services and facilities?

7. Do larger visitor groups (e.g., four or more) participate in different activities than smaller groups?

8. Do frequent visitors rate the overall quality of their park experiences differently than less frequent visitors?

The VSP database website (http://vsp.uidaho.edu) allows data searches for comparisons of data from one or more parks.

For more information please contact:

Visitor Services Project, PSU
College of Natural Resources
875 Perimeter Dr., MS 1139
University of Idaho
Moscow, ID 83843-1139

Phone: 208-885-2585
Fax: 208-885-4261
Email: lenale@uidaho.edu
Website: http://www.psu.uidaho.edu

Appendix 3: Decision Rules for Checking Nonresponse Bias

There are several methods for checking non-response bias. However, the most common way is to use some demographic indicators to compare between respondents and nonrespondents (Dey 1997; Salant and Dillman 1994; Dillman and Carley-Baxter 2000; Dillman, 2007; Stoop 2004). In this study, we used five variable group type, group size, age of the group member (at least 16 years old) completing the survey, whether the park was the primary destination for the visit, and visitor's place of residence proximity to the park to check for nonresponse bias.

Chi-square tests were used to detect the difference in the response rates among different group types, whether the park was the primary destination for this visit, and visitor's place of residence and proximity to the park. The hypothesis was that there is no significant difference across different categories (or groups) between respondents and nonrespondents. If the p-value is greater than 0.05, the difference between respondents and nonrespondents is judged to be insignificant.

Two independent-sample T-tests were used to test the differences between respondent's and nonrespondent's average age and group size. The p-values represent the significance levels of these tests. If p-value is greater than 0.05, the two groups are judged to be insignificantly different.

Therefore, the hypotheses for checking nonresponse bias are:

1. Respondents from different group types are equally represented.

2. Respondents and nonrespondents are not significantly different in terms of proximity from their home to the park.

3. Respondents and nonrespondents are not significantly different in terms of reason for visiting the park.

4. Average age of respondents – average age of nonrespondents = 0.

5. Average group size of respondents – average group size of nonrespondents = 0.

As shown in Tables 2, 3, 4, and 5, the p-value for respondent/nonrespondent comparisons except for group size were less than 0.05, indicating significant differences between respondents and nonrespondents. The results indicate some biases occurred due to nonresponse. Visitors at younger age ranges (especially 35 and younger), came from the local area (within a 50 mile radius), visitors traveling with friends, and visitors indicated park as primary destination to visit the area were underrepresented in the survey results. Results of the study in this report only reflect the simple frequencies. Inferences of the survey results should be weighted to counter balance the effects of nonresponse bias.

References

Dey, E. L. (1997). Working with Low Survey Response Rates: The Efficacy of Weighting Adjustment. *Research in Higher Education*, 38(2): 215-227.

Dillman, D. A. (2007). *Mail and Internet Surveys: The Tailored Design Method, Updated version with New Internet, Visual, and Mixed-Mode Guide*, 2nd Edition, New York: John Wiley and Sons, Inc.

Dillman, D. A. and Carley-Baxter, L. R. (2000). *Structural determinants of survey response rate over a 12-year period, 1988-1999*, Proceedings of the section on survey research methods, 394-399, American Statistical Association, Washington, DC.

Filion, F. L. (Winter 1975-Winter 1976). Estimating Bias due to Non-response in Mail Surveys. *Public Opinion Quarterly*, Vol 39 (4): 482-492.

Goudy, W. J. (1976). Non-response Effect on Relationships Between Variables. *Public Opinion Quarterly*. Vol 40 (3): 360-369.

Mayer, C. S. and Pratt Jr. R. W. (Winter 1966-Winter 1967). A Note on Non-response in a Mail Survey. *Public Opinion Quarterly*. Vol 30 (4): 637-646.

Salant, P. and Dillman, D. A. (1994). *How to Conduct Your Own Survey*. U.S.: John Wiley and Sons, Inc.

Stoop, I. A. L. (2004). Surveying Non-respondents. *Field Methods*, 16 (1): 23.

NPS 178/119304, December 2012

www.ingramcontent.com/pod-product-compliance
Lightning Source LLC
Chambersburg PA
CBHW081457170526

45166CB00008B/2456